Stories From

BEYOND
the EDGE

Books by Sarah Coleman Kelnhofer:

God Who?
Changing Lives

To order, call 1-800-765-6955.
Visit our Web site at www.reviewandherald.com
for information on other Review and Herald
products.

Stories From

BEYOND
the EDGE

Going Where Christ Is Not Known

Sarah Coleman Kelnhofer, editor

REVIEW AND HERALD® PUBLISHING ASSOCIATION
HAGERSTOWN, MD 21740

Adventist Frontier Missions assumes full responsibility for the accuracy
of all facts and quotations as cited in this book.

Unless otherwise noted, Bible texts in this book are from the *Holy Bible, New
International Version.* Copyright © 1973, 1978, 1984, International Bible
Society. Used by permission of Zondervan Bible Publishers.

This book was
Edited by Helen Lee
Copyedited by Jocelyn Fay and James Cavil
Designed by Kimberly Haupt
Cover designed by Kimberly Haupt
Electronic makeup by Shirley M. Bolivar
Typeset: Veljovic Book 11/14

PRINTED IN U.S.A.

05 04 03 02 01   5 4 3 2 1

R&H Cataloging Service
Kelnhofer, Sarah Elizabeth Coleman, 1977-
    Stories from beyond the edge: going where Christ is not known.

    1. Seventh-day Adventists—Missions.   2. Missions—Seventh-day
Adventists.   I. Title

                        266.6732

ISBN 0-8280-1558-9

This book is dedicated to frontier missionaries everywhere, some of whose stories are told here. May your commitment continue to inspire a passion for service in others.

Acknowledgments

I offer my heartfelt thanks to
Glen Wintermeyer, Margie
Mitchell, Tom Toews, Bill
Fagal, Pam Duncan, Clyde
Morgan, Vicki Wiley, and
Chris Kelnhofer for their
generous help in producing
this book.

Contents

Several years ago I became fascinated with frontier missions. At the time, I was working for Adventist Frontier Missions (AFM), and I enjoyed reading the stories that flowed into the magazine, *Adventist Frontiers,* on a regular basis. Each missionary's account of his or her life on the frontier seemed so full of pulse and power, of prayer and passion, that I longed to share their experiences with a wider audience. I believed (and still believe) that the more people know about frontier missions, the more they will become involved in this last-day race to carry the gospel to the world.

This book is a collection of some of the most memorable stories from *Adventist Frontiers.* It has been a joy to read and edit these stories into their present form. I have made every effort to maintain the integrity of the original stories as told by the frontier missionaries themselves. It is my prayer that missionaries (both potential and present) will find inspiration and encouragement in the pages ahead.

—Sarah Coleman Kelnhofer

Frontier Adventures contains 52 stories, making it an ideal source for mission stories at church or Sabbath school, during family worships, or as a personal weekly worship routine.

At the end of each story you will find three sections. Since the audience for this book is so wide, these sections have been written specifically for children (ages 8-15) but can be modified to fit any age group.

• *Get Into the Action* asks thought-provoking questions about the story.

• *Scenario* provides a chance to decide how readers would react in a similar situation.

• *Take Action* gives an opportunity to get involved in real mission/service experience.

In addition to these three sections, you will find informational pages at the beginning of each country section. These pages provide a brief overview of each area and people group featured in the book.

What Is Adventist Frontier Missions?

Adventist Frontier Missions, a supporting ministry of the Seventh-day Adventist church, is a privately funded nonprofit organization, working as an unaffiliated independent ministry operated by Adventist lay members to plant the church among unreached people groups.

If you would like more information about AFM, or missions in general, you may wish to visit AFM's Web site at www.afmonline.org.

Africa

Burkina Faso

⭐Ouagadougou

Burkina Faso: Crowded and in Need

Specs: Sitting in the middle of West Africa, Burkina Faso is one of the poorest and most crowded places in the world. From the jungles in the south, where malaria and "jungle-blindness" threaten, to the bleak deserts of the north, living conditions in Burkina Faso are anything but pleasant for its malnourished people. Like its neighbor Mali, Burkina Faso has rich tribal cultures, game reserves, and deserts.

History: Burkina Faso's name means "the democratic land of men of integrity." Like Mali, Burkina Faso was once ruled by the Mossi kingdom in the middle ages that controlled the trade routes between North and South Africa. The French later set the borders of Burkina Faso, which Mali still disputes today.

People: The Mossi, a farming people, make up Burkina Faso's largest ethnic group. The Mande, Bobo, and Lobi are also unique cultures to Burkina Faso. Lobi farmers and hunters govern themselves traditionally through the clan system. The Lobi were purely animists until Islamic influence entered the area. The Lobi men practice polygamy by marrying several wives.

Village boys enjoy playing with homemade wire cars.

DID YOU KNOW . . .

• It's against the law to photograph anything or anyone that is part of Burkina Faso's government. Anyone taking a picture of people should ask their permission first.

• It's rude to shake hands with the locals in the north if you're a woman.

• In Ouagadougou, the capital of Burkina Faso, one of the best ways to get around is on a bicycle. On any given day you'll see thousands in the streets.

• Bring bug repellent! There are thousands of mosquitoes and flies, even inside houses.

• Monday and Thursday afternoons are sports afternoons, 23 and many offices are closed.

Children often sit by the road and sell their wares.

Grandma Fossirana

Unafraid of Change By Margret Unglaub

"Margaret, come outside!" Kurt Unglaub's voice carried indoors to where Margaret was busily unpacking her family's belongings. "I want you to meet someone."

Margaret quickly set down the load of clothes she had in her arms. It was her first week in Africa, and already Kurt had introduced her to more people than she could possibly remember! Their names rang in her ears like strange-sounding songs, and she almost shuddered at the thought of adding another one to the list.

Still, she thought as she pushed open the screen door, *we're here to make friends with the Lobi people. I'm happy to meet another person.*

"Margaret, this is Fossirana." Kurt's voice held a touch of amusement as he introduced the tiny brown woman beside him. "While I was preparing our home for you and the kids, she visited me nearly every day. She has been eager to meet you."

"I'm so pleased to meet you," Margaret said in her halting Lobiri dialect. She had no idea that they would see so much of each other in the years to come.

Almost every day Fossirana stopped in "for a short visit" with Margaret. And almost every day she stayed at least an hour. She was thin and wiry, and Margaret could tell that she'd spent a long life working in the fields. Now, too old to work and too proud to beg, Fossirana relied on the generosity of her friends and family to provide for her needs. She quickly became known as the Unglaubs' "Lobi grandmother" and took pride in her new White family.

Fossirana did not know how old she was—some said 76 or 78 years of age, but there was no way to know for sure. Her stooped shoulders and calloused hands showed that she had lived a difficult life even by Lobi standards. Her two sons had moved long ago to Côte d'Ivoire (Ivory Coast), leaving promises but no money. When the Unglaubs met her she had been gathering what food she could but had become too weak to plant her own fields. Fossirana was completely dependent upon the goodwill of her neighbors.

In Lobi culture food is given first to the young and healthy, who can earn their keep. Elderly people are respected in words, but when it comes to food and material comforts, they are too often passed by. This system often forces the elderly to resort to begging. Fossirana hadn't quite reached this stage, and she'd never reach it if she could help it! She often hinted of her needs for food or clothing.

For a while the Unglaubs asked their friends to cook rice and sauce for her while improving their own open-fire cooking skills. They often gave her extra food from their table or shared their garden produce. Once Fossirana's leaky mud roof had to be fixed, and the church members paid for its repair.

Margaret's friendship with Fossirana continued for several years. But one dry season, while Fossirana recovered from an especially serious illness, Margaret became concerned that Fossirana would die not really knowing Jesus or having hope in her heart.

Margaret took matters into her own hands. "Bebe," she asked a village boy who wandered in while Fossirana was visiting, "can you tell Fossirana about Jesus in her own language? I don't speak Lobiri well enough to do it myself, and I want her to fully understand who He is."

Bebe nodded and began talking to Fossirana immediately.

After listening patiently to his speech, Fossirana nodded her graying head. "I will accept Jesus in my life. The fetishes [objects believed to hold magical powers] never did a thing for me. I didn't believe in them."

Bebe grinned from ear to ear. A convert! He'd won a convert for Jesus! But Margaret wasn't so sure. It all seemed too easy . . . too simple to be true.

After another church member gave Fossirana several weeks of Bible studies, he felt sure that she understood the good news of Jesus. "Just believe it, Margaret," he told her with a grin. "She understands!"

Margaret's heart filled with joy. It was true! Her beloved Grandma Fossirana had become a real member of her eternal family!

Most older Africans do not easily change from their traditional ways. A typical response is "I am too old now. It's OK for the young folks, but I am just too old." Fossirana, however, was not afraid of change. She began coming to church every Sabbath and memorizing Bible verses faster than many of the younger members. She now sings Lobiri gospel songs, prays, or recites scripture while she works around her house.

But Fossirana wouldn't be completely content until the fetish objects were removed from her home and courtyard. Not long after she began attending church regularly Kurt agreed to help her with the project. He convinced several African boys to help him that very evening. They were a little frightened of desecrating something considered supernatural, but agreed to go in faith.

When they finished, they dedicated Fossirana's house to God. The next day the young men sighed in wonder that nothing had happened. No harm had fallen upon them or the home. They were surprised, but not Fossirana.

"I believe in God!" she proclaimed courageously. "Nothing is stronger than He is!"

Grandma Fossirana has always been Margaret's cheerleader and encourager, but now more than ever she is cheerful and caring when it comes to other people. She has an indomitable spirit spiked with Lobi humor that brings lots of laughs around the cooking fire.

This change in her character was a witness to another animist in the village, who saw that leaving the fetishes had caused Fossirana no harm. The woman was amazed at how happy and honest Fossirana had become. She recently told her grandson, "I think I'd like to go to your church too. If Fossirana can do it, so can I."

Get Into the Action!

1. How do the Lobi people view the elderly? Why do you think this is?
2. In the beginning why do you think Fossirana was so eager to befriend the Unglaubs? How did they help her with her physical needs?
3. Read Matthew 4:4 and John 6:35. What did Fossirana need more than anything else?
4. Why do you think it was easy for her to accept the Christian way when so many people her age say they are "too old"?

Scenario

You know John is hungry. Every day his lunch seems smaller than it was the day before. It's always the same—a white bread sandwich and a bottle of pop. He doesn't concentrate well in school, and you know it's because he's not getting healthy food. Several times you've seen him eyeing your own large tasty lunch.

How can you help him without making him feel bad?

There are many ways to reach out to people around you. One important kind of outreach is called "physical outreach." This includes medical work in foreign countries or inner cities, feeding ministries, volunteer work for the elderly or the sick, tutoring, etc. Physical outreach involves anything that helps a person's immediate physical needs. Talk with a parent or guardian about how you might be able to get involved in physical outreach in your community. Then take action and begin your outreach project. If it turns out to be a success, get your school or Sabbath school class involved.

Jesus' life is a perfect example of physical outreach. Skim through the Gospels (Matthew, Mark, Luke, and John) and notice all the different times Jesus physically helped other people. Make a pledge that looks something like this:

Jesus healed the widow's son. *I will visit my uncle in the hospital.*

Jesus fed the 5,000. *I will invite friends to my house to eat.*

In this story Fossirana's age put her at a disadvantage in the village. Even though our society values older people, they sometimes feel neglected. Look around your church and notice which older people seem lonely or alone. Do something special for each of them in the next several months. (Or visit a nursing home, take cards or food to elderly shut-ins, etc.)

Pale Phinyale and Kurt Unglaub

I would like to be a Christian and become a member of your church," Pale Phinyale (pronounced Palay Phinlalay) blurted out to Kurt and Margaret Unglaub. He could tell by the surprised looks on their faces that they weren't used to hearing this from total strangers who were dusty and disheveled from miles of hiking through the dry bush. But he didn't care. He'd been planning on becoming a Christian for years now.

"Pale," Kurt began carefully, "we are very happy to hear that you'd like to join our church. But we'd like to know a little bit about you! Is that all right?"

Pale nodded and squatted next to them on the floor. "I come from Sanmbitera, many hours from here."

Margaret gasped. "Such a hike! You look tired and hungry. Can I get you something to eat?"

Again Pale nodded. He continued his story while Margaret bustled around in the kitchen. "My village is like most other African villages," he began slowly. "Everybody worships the fetishes. We have no schools, no clean water to drink, and usually not enough food to go around. Fights break out all the time among families and friends, and we trust the spirits to solve our problems."

"Do the spirits help?" Kurt asked quietly.

Pale had a feeling that Kurt already knew the answer. "No, my village is unhappy and poor as always. Everyone, even the children, drinks millet beer. Several years ago I realized that I was unhappy and that I was not on a good road. I think the spirits are to blame."

Pale accepted a heaping bowl of rice and vegetables from Margaret and began to eat ravenously. The missionaries smiled and let him eat while they waited for him to continue his story.

"Many times since then I have promised myself to get rid of my fetishes and become a Christian," Pale said with a full mouth. "I know several Christian families, and they seem happier than I am. But," he waved a rice-covered hand in the air, "my promises were lies. Every time the day arrived that I had vowed to destroy my fetishes, I couldn't do it." He smiled broadly. "Until today. I want to be a Christian and join your church. I want to leave my old life behind."

Kurt and Margaret stared in awe at this tall African. Had he really hiked through the bush all morning to tell them this? Carefully they explained what it meant to be a Christian, told Pale when their church met, and prayed a simple prayer with him. Several hours later a grinning Pale hiked back into the bush—his home was 12 miles (20 kilometers) away.

"Think we'll see him again?" Margaret asked as she cleared away the dishes from Pale's meal.

"Hard to tell." Kurt stared at Pale's retreating back. "He seemed pretty excited."

In the weeks that followed, Pale proved just how serious he was. The very next Sabbath he arrived, on time, with one of his wives and their child. After the service they happily made the 12-mile (20-kilometer) hike back to their village. The next Sabbath the whole family came!

By the end of that year Pale cleared his house and courtyard of all his old fetishes. God also worked miracles to reduce the number of wives in his house from three to one! And almost every Sabbath all, or at least part, of Pale's large extended family makes the dusty trek to the church in Loropeni.

But has all this effort made any difference in Pale's life? Life in Lobiland is still hard. Most of his village still drink millet beer and fight over food and water. But Pale's heart has changed. He has peace and joy because he knows his sins are forgiven. He has a strong hope for the future—a future when water, food, and millet beer will be the least of his concerns. A future when God will welcome him into a heavenly village.

1. Why do you think Pale had a hard time keeping his promises about getting rid of his fetishes?
2. Read Matthew 26:41. How does the verse apply to Pale's story?
3. Who were the biggest positive Christian influences in Pale's life? Do you think they were native families? If so, how do you think they heard about Jesus?
4. What responsibility does that give us as Christians? (Read Matthew 28:19, 20.)

One day you hear a knock at the door. When you answer it, you find yourself standing face-to-face with a woman who looks homeless. She is bedraggled and covered in dirt. She doesn't smell very good, either. But her eyes are honest and sincere, and she smiles at you warmly.

"I want to be a Christian," she tells you simply. You learn that one of your neighbors met her in the city and directed her to your house, telling her that you are a Christian and could help her.

How will you respond?

There are probably hundreds of people out there who are just like Pale. They want to become Christians and give up bad habits, but they have a hard time mustering up enough willpower to change. Unfortunately, you may not always know who these people are. How can you reach them anyway?

Make a list of ways you can live your life so that people who know you will also want to become Christians. Take your ideas from the lives of some great Christian examples around you—people who make Christianity appealing and fun.

Tell the people whose ideas you listed that you are thankful for their positive example. Ask them if they have any more good ideas for living a joyful Christian life.

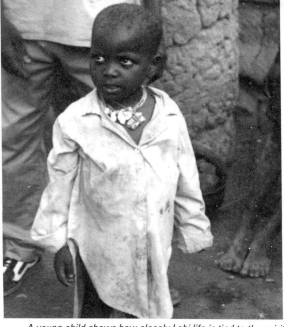

3

A young child shows how closely Lobi life is tied to the spirit world. Superstitious parents make their children wear strings and charms to prevent sickness or a bad spirit from coming over them and to ensure good life and good character.

Kurt Unglaub held his spoon poised in front of his mouth, like an airplane waiting to land. He stared over its cargo of rice at Pale's worried face. *Another emergency,* he thought wryly. *So much for a quiet breakfast.*

"Please come," Pale finally spoke. "Minata is having trouble breathing."

Kurt glanced at his wife, Margaret. Her breakfast forgotten, she had already moved from the table and picked up her shiny stethoscope.

"Let's hurry," she said simply.

Minata, a younger member of the village, was as dear to their hearts as a family member. She must be cared for.

Pale silently led Kurt and Margaret toward Minata's hut. Once they entered her courtyard, he added the words that shocked them both. "Actually, she's had this trouble with evil spirits before."

Evil spirits? Kurt's mind whirled frantically. *This may be more complicated than I thought!*

A wrinkled woman met them at the door and

"Call Unto Me"

By Kurt Unglaub

25

clutched at Kurt's arm. "Can you help her? Can you help her? Oh, my poor granddaughter!"

"We'll do our best," Kurt mumbled, his attention already focused on the sleeping mat in the corner. There three muscular-looking women had Minata pinned to the floor, her arms held down by their ample weight. Kurt was about to ask why the restraint was necessary when Minata let forth a terrible scream.

"Auuuuuggh!" she shrieked at the top of her lungs. Her body writhed beneath the three women, and her muscles strained to be free. The screaming continued, interspersed with eerie laughter. Finally Minata quieted down. Only the heavy breathing of the three sweating women filled the hut.

By this time both Kurt and Margaret had begun to sweat as well. Wordlessly Margaret dropped her stethoscope to the ground. It wouldn't be needed today. A look passed between Kurt and Margaret as they searched for a solution to Minata's demonic problem.

While Kurt continued to think, Margaret dropped to her knees and began stroking Minata's hot forehead and repeating her name like a song. "Minata, Minata, Miiinaaataaa." Minata answered with another gut-bursting scream, then a laugh.

We have got to establish contact with her! Kurt realized as he watched the scene unfold. *We can't let Satan take control of this girl!*

But poor Minata could do nothing but scream in response to their calls. Her mind was far away, in the possession of a power no one knew quite how to reckon with. She seemed to be trapped in a nightmare, and nothing the worried missionaries did could bring her out of it.

It didn't take long to run out of ideas. Minata showed no sign of coming around or letting up, and her grandmother had begun to wail in the background. The hut's dim interior suddenly seemed darker with the presence of Minata's evil spirit.

Kurt dropped to his knees beside his wife. "Lord," he began shakily, "there's nothing we can do here. If anything is going to happen, it's got to come from You."

Pale, who had stayed by to help, murmured a soft "Amen."

Margaret squeezed her husband's hand. They urgently needed supernatural help.

"Father," Kurt continued, encouraged by their support, "please accept us as Your agents of love to reach Minata. We know we are unworthy of this miracle, but we pray on behalf of Minata. Please, Lord, work a miracle for her sake. Save her from the power of the devil. Deliver Minata from Satan! In Your holy name, amen."

"Amen," echoed Pale.

"Amen," murmured Margaret from her position next to Minata. Before even opening her eyes, Margaret knew something was different. Minata's body had relaxed! Her eyes no longer held a glazed expression. She blinked a few times and gazed up at the ring of faces surrounding her mat.

"What are you staring at?" she demanded. "Can I please have my baby?"

The three women who had been holding Minata shook their heads in disbelief. Could it be? They were so overwhelmed that they forgot to let Minata stand up! She began to prod them and, surprised, they released their grip on her arms.

She stood up, stretched, and gazed around the circle again. "What are you staring at?" she repeated.

Kurt felt goose bumps forming on his arms and neck. "We're staring at a miracle," he whispered softly, in awe of the God he served.

Kurt and Margaret rose to leave, still shaking their heads in wonder. Just as everyone left the room for the courtyard, a Muslim exorcist arrived. "Your services will not be needed here," Minata's grandmother told him proudly. "Minata is just fine."

Suddenly Kurt felt the desire to speak. He cleared his throat and sent a silent prayer heavenward for the words to say.

"Jesus has done a wonderful things for Minata just now," Kurt began carefully. He didn't want to trample on the feelings of the many Muslims who were present. They seemed to be interested, so he continued. "But we should pray that God will not allow the evil spirits to return."

There was no debate and no hesitation as at least 12 pairs of legs knelt in the presence of God and the many angels present. Jesus Christ alone was on center stage!

Before long Minata drifted into a deep and peaceful sleep. Kurt and Margaret gathered their medical equipment and left the hut, headed back home for a now-cold breakfast.

I don't mind this kind of interruption, Kurt thought as they crossed the street for the second time that morning. Together he and Margaret praised God for his presence that morning.

"Call to Me, and I will answer you, and show you great and mighty things, which you do not know" (Jeremiah 33:3, NKJV).

Get Into the Action!

1. Why do you think Minata's grandmother believed Kurt and Margaret might be able to help? After all, she was a Muslim and they were Christians.
2. Read Luke 10:17-20. Even though Kurt and Margaret rejoiced in the fact that God was able to use them, what should they rejoice in even more?

Scenario

Your friend is sick and in the hospital. You and your pastor pray with her and her family, and she feels better within several days. She begins telling everyone at school that you are a "miracle worker."

What should you do?

Take Action!

Ask your pastor about intercessory prayer.

Try praying specifically for a person or situation for a long period of time (at least one month). Record your thoughts and the results of this "experiment."

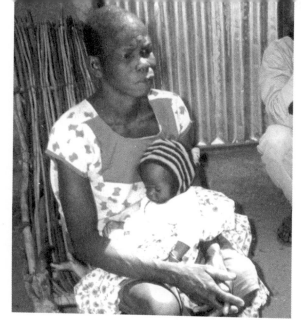

A Lobi mother and her child

4

Rina straightened her back and forced her aching feet to carry her forward. "No, Lord!" she pleaded in misery. "Please don't let my children die!"

Rina had been on a trip when a murderous tropical rainstorm had struck her small African village. Seized with fear at the news of the storm, she had immediately begun traveling toward home.

The closer she came to her village, the worse the damage was. Trees lay uprooted in the trail, their roots pointing skyward like accusing fingers. Branches, connected only by their bark, dangled from the trunks of tattered trees. The sounds of wailing rose from each village she passed.

"Have you heard any news of my village?" she asked every person she met on the trail.

Inevitably the answer was the same. "It's bad in your village, grandmother. Very, very bad." Now, as she trudged the last few miles toward home, Rina's hopes sank lower and lower. Would she find the entire village in shambles? Would her children be injured be-

Saved! By Kurt Unglaub

29

yond recognition? What about little Lisa? Had her brothers and sisters taken care of her during the long windy night?

Rina shuddered. Leftover droplets of rain from the storm mixed with the hot tears coursing down her cheeks. She felt tired, alone, and afraid. Could she face the future without her children?

Rina stopped and stared up at the sky in despair. Angry black clouds seethed above her, and she wondered if another storm were brewing.

"Father God, please rescue my children!" she pleaded.

The rain continued to fall, but a slight opening in the clouds revealed a scrap of blue sky. Rina caught her breath. God had heard her. She knew that He loved her and that He would watch over her even if every one of her children had died in the storm.

With new resolve Rina continued her journey. Her heart beat faster and faster as she climbed the final hill toward her village. The mud sucked at her bare feet and covered her cane, but she plodded resolutely forward.

Now she could see the smoke from a few cooking fires. The outskirts of the village came into view, and she stared, white-faced, at the spot where her hut should have been. It was gone!

Her courage forgotten, Rina hobbled down the hill, wailing at the top of her lungs. "My babies, my babies, my babies!"

Rina longed for a warm embrace from someone—from anyone who could comfort her as she surveyed the wreckage that used to be her home. She knew that her children lay lifeless under the fallen wood and bricks. She should have known better.

"Rina," one neighbor hissed as she stumbled by, "look what your Jesus has done for you!" His wrinkled face broke into a cruel grin. "Do you trust Him now? Do you? Do you?"

Rina squelched her wails, wiped her eyes, and looked back at him. "I do," she said simply, remembering the blue sky He had shown her. "My Jesus will not desert me."

"Rina, Rina!" The other villagers took up the torture. "We knew this would happen. You prayed to this strange God, and see the results? Maybe this will teach you not to defy the fetishes!" They were merciless.

Rina tried to ignore the nauseating pain in her heart as she summoned up a reply from the Bible. "The Lord giveth, the Lord taketh away. I will trust Him as long as I live. I will pray anyway. We will see what God can do."

The men began clearing away the heavy crumbled mud walls. Their backs strained as they lifted the large chunks into a new pile. Rina gasped as one man lifted away a huge piece of wall. One tiny brown leg showed from beneath the rubbish. The man pulled roughly on the leg and finally succeeded in freeing Lisa from the wreckage.

Rina began to cry, but her tears soon turned to tears of joy. Lisa, her "dead" little daughter, stood up!

"I'm thirsty," she complained in a raspy little voice. "Can I have some water?"

"God be praised!" Rina sang, enveloping her surprised little girl in a tight hug. "You're alive!"

The men moving the rubbish were too stunned to speak. By now Rina's neighbors stood at a respectful distance from the rejoicing woman and her daughter. No insults interrupted the silence now. Only the sound of large plaster walls scraping against each other could be heard in the African twilight.

Soon a second set of legs emerged, followed by a living, breathing little boy. Johnny too was unscathed by the massive brick walls. By the end of the evening every single one of Rina's children had been rescued. And every single one was alive and uninjured.

Rina, tears of joy streaming down her wrinkled old face, held them all to her and offered a heartfelt prayer of thanks to her faithful Father God. Needless to say, Rina has never again been criticized because of her religion.

1. Who else said, "The Lord gave and the Lord has taken away"? Find the place in the Bible, and read the character's story.
2. What do you think would have happened if Rina's children had died instead of surviving the storm?
3. How could God have used Rina as an example to the villagers even if her children had died?

You've always wanted a new bike, and you finally receive one for your birthday. Several weeks later you come home to discover that someone has stolen it. In spite of your sadness, what can you do to show others that God is still the most important thing in your life?

Read the obituary section in the newspaper. Make cards for the surviving members of the deceased person's family, and mail them as soon as possible. If you know someone who has lost a friend or family member recently, deliver a card in person.

Do you have any miracle stories of your own? Has God saved your life or the life of someone you know? Have you told many people about it? This week, tell at least three people about God's goodness to you.

Caroline Nicola and a Lobi friend

I was there the day it all started. Caroline Nicola, my owner, burst into the room, picked me up, and flipped through my pages. Then she sank into the nearest chair and read to herself, "Go into all the world and preach the good news to all creation" (Mark 16:15).

She gently set me down on the cluttered table beside her and commented to no one in particular, "I guess that includes Burkina Faso."

All that scorching summer she opened me often, pouring through my chapters about Paul's missionary journeys. I could tell we were working up to something, and it wasn't long until I found out just what that something was.

On the big day I sat in a place of honor on top of a stack of clean T-shirts and watched as she stuffed more and more things into a suitcase. Just when I thought it would pop, she forced it closed, zipped it up, and turned to tuck me into her backpack.

I stayed in there for what seemed like forever when suddenly a hand rummaged around in the backpack, and a dark face peered into the opening. Where was I? All around I heard people talking excitedly in a strange language. As the sun beat down on my open pages, I suddenly realized my owner and I had reached our destination: Burkina Faso, West Africa!

The next few months weren't easy. My creases filled with dirt, dust, and mosquitoes, and my once-smooth pages began to wrinkle from the humidity. My owner opened me often, and I heard her talking quietly to my Author. Sometimes she cried big drops of salt water onto my pages, but she always cheered up when she read, "Be strong and take heart, all you who hope in the Lord" (Psalm 31:24).

Now, every Sabbath my owner smiles when little brown hands tug me out of her grasp and turn carefully through my upside-down pages. Often she takes me across town to visit a friend.

Many memorable months have passed since then, and I realize I'm not as shiny as I used to be. My cover's becoming worn, and sometimes my pages crackle noisily when they're turned. But overall, I am a pretty happy book. I know my Author would be proud of me.

Get Into the Action!

1. Who is the speaker in this story? What can you tell about the owner of the book from this story? How does she feel about her Bible?
2. What does the Bible have to say for itself in these verses?
   Hebrews 4:12
   Proverbs 30:5
   Psalm 119:105
   Psalm 119:111
3. Is it a good or a bad thing that Caroline's Bible was worn out by the end of the year?

Scenario

I am your Bible. I sit in your bookcase day after day and watch you bustle around your room. Often you have friends who visit you, but you never talk about me. I want you to read me. I want to help you get to know my Author. But I can only be silent until you pick me up.

Sometimes you open my pages and read for a few minutes, but you never establish any sort of strong pattern. I want you to spend time with me on a regular basis.

What will you do?

Read Psalm 119:9-16. This section of the Bible is a good reminder of all the reasons we should spend time reading God's Word. Write it out neatly on a decorated sheet of paper and put it on your wall to remind you to read the Bible. Memorize the section or put it to music like David did when he wrote it.

Read your Bible! Make it fun! Share your discoveries with others. Here are some ideas to get you going.

Color in your Bible! Use those old crayons to highlight special verses. You can use this system or make your own.

> Promises: Green
> Warnings: Blue
> Praise/Thanks: Yellow
> Prophecy: Red
> Instructions: Orange

Press flowers in your Bible.

Write verses on note cards and use them as bookmarks in your Bible.

Take notes on sermons and keep them in your Bible.

Write all over in your Bible! Underline or make notes in the margins about particular verses, You can even jot quick notes to God—"Thank You" or "I love You" or "Help me to be like this" or any number of things. Including the date every time you write a note in your Bible will make it like a special diary of your spiritual journey.

Memorize Bible verses with friends.

Set the Bible to music.

Put your name into verses that fit.

Read the Bible out loud.

Read several different versions of the Bible.

Use a concordance.

Talk about what you read with other people.

Use your imagination!

Think of a missionary you know. (If you don't know anyone overseas, think of a person in your area who does mission work—a pastor, teacher, or volunteer.) Search your Bible for texts that would encourage that person. Write them out neatly and mail them, along with an encouraging note, to the missionary.

Begin a list of "strength texts" that will give you courage and support in tough situations. Keep the list in your Bible.

Sie, his wife and child, and Kurt Unglaub

6

Searching for a Saviour

By Kurt Unglaub

Sie shook his head to clear it. "Where am I going?" he mumbled to himself. He had no answer. Last night had nearly done him in—too much millet beer had left him reeling for hours. In fact, he wasn't even sure he was awake. But after closing his eyes and opening them again, Sie realized he couldn't be sleeping. The vivid blue sky arched above him like a huge silk tent. Baobob trees stood against the horizon like wizened old men, and countless African birds hooted at him from their gnarled branches.

Sie stopped and looked around. He remembered where he was headed—the local liquor store—but his feet were directing him elsewhere! The scenery around him told him he was going in the opposite direction of the store. Still half-conscious, Sie decided to follow this strange impulse and see where it led him. *After all,* he reasoned in a sudden moment of clarity, *it can't be worse than where I've been.*

Born in Bobo Dioulasso around 1958, Sie was the son of a Lobi medicine man. He remembered his father using divinations to give counsel, prescribe cures, and settle disputes for countless confused villagers. His father both feared and respected the fetishes, the objects believed to have magical powers. At a very early age Sie determined not to follow in his father's footsteps. He'd seen too much of the fetishes darker side, and he didn't want to get involved.

So Sie studied to become a mason, and it was a proud day when he attained his license and took it home to show his family. He launched a successful career, spending his newfound riches on liquor and prostitutes.

And then his memories grew foggy. He knew that spirits had begun to appear to him. He vaguely remembered their shadowy forms approaching him, their arms raised threateningly above his head. Every time he sat down a new spirit would rush angrily toward him. Sie had discovered that the moment he stood up the spirits would disappear. Soon Sie realized that unless he kept moving, the spirits would appear again. He began to wander the streets in a daze. Voices began telling him that if he got too near crowds of people they would kill him. Thus, if he found himself with more than one person at a time, he would panic. To avoid people, Sie began living alone in the bush. He was unable to work or to function in society, and he couldn't stop moving.

Sie began walking that summer, he knew that much for sure. He vaguely remembered the great distances he had covered— literally hundreds of miles on foot between Burkina Faso and the Ivory Coast. He actually walked the soles off his own feet, yet he kept on for three years. He slept in the bush or in cemeteries, anywhere to avoid contact with people. He became known as the "crazy man." His clothes rotted off his body, and his hair became a stringy, matted mess. There were times when his reason would return for a while, and he would say in his mind, "God, if you're there, don't leave me like this."

After one such prayer, Sie began to feel a change in his mind. The spirits chased him less and less frequently. Gradually, Sie's sanity returned. He resumed his work and became even more successful than before. Unfortunately, he also resumed all his old, bad habits. This eventually drove him to leave his job and return to his ancestral village, Loropeni. "Maybe life will be easier in the village of my ancestors," Sie had hoped.

But Loropeni offered no perfect life for Sie. By now he had a wife and child and was barely able to make ends meet. He did small construction jobs and odd work but always ended up spending his money on the local millet beer.

Sie jerked to consciousness. He'd been daydreaming as his feet led him along a dusty path through the village. He kicked at a tree root in the trail. *I'm not sure where I'm going,* he thought miserably, *but it doesn't matter any more. My life is hopeless.*

Suddenly Sie's feet stopped moving. He stared at his wide brown toes for a moment, then ventured his gaze a little higher. A neat house stood in front of him. The sound of laughter and cheerful voices drifted out on the afternoon breeze. On an impulse, Sie walked in the front door and sat on the first patch of open floor he came to.

Kurt Unglaub, who had been about to wind down his prayer meeting talk for the evening, saw Sie enter and decided to continue a little longer. Thank God he did! By the end of the evening, Sie had given his tired heart to Christ. Running no more, he sat in the tiny missionary home with tears streaming down his face. He knew his life would never be the same.

1. Why do you think Sie was especially vulnerable to attacks from evil spirits?
2. Read Matthew 12:43-45. How does this explain why Sie went back to drinking rice liquor after the evil spirits left him?
3. How do you think Sie's life changed after his conversion?

Your friend has read dirty books for several years now. After talking with you, he decides to throw away all of his books and start a new, clean life. What else should you tell him to do? (Hint: Read the text from Question 2 above.)

1. Make a list of the bad habits you have and think about what is stopping you from breaking these habits. Pray for God to give you the willpower to change. If you feel comfortable, tell a friend and ask him or her to pray with you.
2. Kurt had to be very in tune with God to realize that he should continue his meeting after Sie entered his house. Think about staying in tune with God and how you can hear His voice.

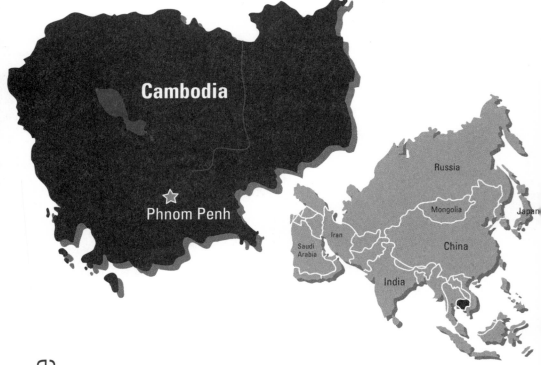

Cambodia: Seeking Peace

Specs: Still recovering from a devastating past, Cambodia continues to seek peace. This southeastern Asian country is home to political insects, snakes, humidity, and heat. Most people in Cambodia belong to a mostly Buddhist group called the Khmer.

History: In the late 1970s the Khmer Rouge, a militant guerrilla group, came to power and drove virtually all urban dwellers into the countryside. They hoped to transform Cambodia into an agricultural giant. In the process, the Khmer Rouge murdered almost all of Cambodia's educated class and over one-quarter of the population (over 2 million people) in mass graves called "killing fields." Although Cambodia longs for peace, the Khmer Rouge still causes political instability.

People: The Khmer are a predominantly agricultural people. They eat plenty of rice and fish and live in villages of several hundred persons. To make money, the Khmer weave, make pottery, and work with metal. They live in wood or concrete houses with gabled roofs. Households are based on the nuclear family and occasionally include other close relatives. The Khmer follow Theravada Buddhism and the use of magic to ward off bad influences.

Cambodian children often wear special necklaces to keep away evil spirits.

DID YOU KNOW?

• Some Cambodians live in floating villages and others raise crocodiles!

• Angkor Wat is one of the finest temples in the world, but don't wander too far because mines were laid to keep Khmer Rouge guerrillas and archeological poachers away.

• In the cities tricycle rickshaws and scooter taxis are the primary means of travel.

• Tonlesap Lake is the largest lake in Southeast Asia and provides water for much of Cambodia. During the dry season the water is so shallow natives grow rice in the lakebed, but during the monsoon season water reaches almost 45 feet deep!

Even little boys are allowed to become Buddhist monks.

Camera

7

Obstacles By Stacey Hooker

"It can't be true." Julie shook her head and forced the bad news from her mind, but Scott persisted.

"Listen, Julie. It is true. A church member told me today. The government has decided that every student will be required to attend classes on Saturday."

"But . . . but . . ." Julie crossed her arms. "They can't do that!"

"I wish they couldn't." Scott settled onto the floor beside his wife. They were both thinking of Camera, one of their very first church members, and the other young people in the church. Would they be strong enough to stand for the Sabbath?

"This is going to be tough," Scott told Julie carefully. "Camera's parents have told him that he has to go to school on Saturday. Along with the government, that makes two huge obstacles to Camera's faith."

Julie sighed. "I know. It's so important for Cambodians to honor their parents. Poor Camera! He must feel torn in two!"

When Camera came by to visit Scott and Julie the

next day, he had a worried look on his face. "If my parents ask me to disobey the Ten Commandments, I won't," he said. "It will be very hard, though. Maybe I should just skip classes and suffer my parents' punishment."

Julie frowned. "I don't know, Camera. What would your parents think about Christianity if you did that? They'd think your new religion had taught you to disobey your parents. They might become very angry with Scott and me and forbid you to come to church." She traced her finger along a pattern on her dress. "I'm sure there's a better way to solve this."

"Maybe," Camera said with a sigh, "but we're running out of time!"

"We'll do the best we can," Scott said. "And we'll leave the rest up to God. Tomorrow we're going to sort things out. Please pray while we're gone."

Camera nodded, said his goodbyes, and left for the night.

The next day, after some serious soul-searching and prayer, Scott, Julie, and two other helpers set out on their mission. They were sent from office to office and eventually ended up at the door of Camera's schoolmaster's office. "If we can get his permission for Camera to be absent on Saturdays," Scott whispered before pushing the door open, "the higher officials will approve it. And maybe Camera's parents will too."

"I know why you're here," Camera's schoolmaster informed the small party of foreigners after they were seated. "And I'm afraid I can't help you." His eyebrows arched up in an expression of pity. "If Camera doesn't attend school on Saturdays, he will be counted absent. If he misses tests and fails classes, he simply cannot take the year-end test." The schoolmaster clasped his hands and laid them gently on the desk. "I'm sorry, but the answer is no."

Scott took a deep breath and told the schoolmaster the reasons he believed Camera should be allowed to skip classes. Julie did the same. With a growing feeling of hopelessness, the other two helpers followed their example. After each small speech the schoolmaster's decision remained the same.

As the small group stood up to go, Julie realized how hope-

Camera at his baptism

less the situation was if they couldn't even cross the first obstacle. *Camera's parents will never consent without the schoolmaster's approval.* Julie sent up one last plea for God to change the schoolmaster's mind. She flashed him her most winning smile and asked once again for Camera's freedom.

To her surprise the schoolmaster smiled back at her. "OK," he answered simply, "you've convinced me. He can skip classes on Saturdays."

Needless to say, Julie nearly shouted for joy. One obstacle crossed!

"Now we have to deal with Camera's parents," Scott reminded Julie on the way home.

"God can change their minds," she told him confidently. "Just wait and see." Nothing could dim her enthusiasm.

Several days before school was scheduled to begin, Camera told Scott and Julie that he was going to talk with his parents that night. "Please pray for me," he begged them. "I'll need all the help I can get."

Both Scott and Julie prayed and fasted that evening. They could hardly sleep that night and answered Camera's knock the next morning with fear and trepidation. Had God proved Himself for Camera?

"Good morning," Camera greeted them quietly. His head hung low as he entered the room.

Julie's heart sank. "They said no?"

Suddenly Camera's frown turned into a smile, and he began jumping up and down in excitement. "They said yes! They said yes! I was just teasing you with my frown!"

Camera's mother had been upset the night before, so he had waited until the morning to talk with her. After listening to his request in silence, she had consented—with a stern warning that he had better pass the year-end exam.

"I just know I can pass!" he told Scott and Julie. "If God has helped me this far, He won't let me down now!"

Scott and Julie grinned at each other. Yes indeed, God had proved Himself strong to Camera. Why had they ever doubted Him?

1. Why did Scott and Julie feel that they should talk to the schoolmaster before Camera approached his parents?
2. Why was Camera's example so important to the future of the church in Cambodia?
3. Why do you think Julie decided to ask the schoolmaster one more time before she left his office?
4. Read Proverbs 21:1. How does this verse apply to Camera's story?

You stare up at the office door, unsure if you should enter the room or run for your life. "Howard A. Mannis, Principal," the plaque reads. You've been sent here by your teacher for refusing to attend a play for class on Sabbath afternoon. You know Mr. Mannis has a reputation for his short temper, and you'd rather not upset him, but you just don't feel right about going to the play.

You waver in front of his door, weighing your options, before you finally make a decision. *What will you decide, and why?*

Read and memorize Psalm 37:5 or Isaiah 30:21.

Think of a time when Jesus went against the wishes of His family or the authorities of the day. Why did He do it? Why was it OK?

Pray for the people of Cambodia, that they may experience more religious freedom in the future. Thank God for the free country you live in.

Joelle Griswold and Tah love to play together.

8

Scott Griswold glanced anxiously at the bright-red stocking hanging on the wall next to his family's usual four. Stitched across the top, the name "Tah" stood out in bold contrast to the American names sewed on the other stockings.

"When is he coming?" 4-year-old Joelle demanded, impatiently pressing her nose against the window. "Will he be here soon?"

"I think so," Scott promised. He scooped 1-year-old Nathan from the floor and went to stand by Joelle at the window. "He'll be so excited to see all his presents!"

Joelle giggled. Scott's wife, Julie, agreed from the kitchen. Even Nathan seemed caught up in the excitement. The members of the Griswold family had a soft spot in their hearts for their little friend Tah. Scott let his mind drift back to their first meeting nine months ago.

While they were in Thailand waiting for Nathan to be born, the Griswolds' student missionary had written to inform them that their house had become a hideout for a small orphan boy. "An old grandmother found him on the street, selling cakes and candies for a cruel man who owned him," the student missionary wrote. "Needless to say, she whisked him away to safety—and hid him in your house!"

By the time the Griswolds got home, however, Tep Ro Tah was out of the house. He had gone to live with the grandmother woman in her almost underground shack beside the railroad tracks. He seemed happy enough, eating rice three times a day and following his protector around as she sold bits of bark for traditional medicinal teas. When Tah came by one day to meet the Griswolds, they became instant friends.

"Scott, I can't believe he's 12!" Julie lamented when she saw him for the first time. "He barely looks 8!"

Polite and quiet, Tah graciously accepted some badly needed clothes. The Griswolds slowly learned his story.

Tah's parents had gotten divorced when he was little. When his mother had remarried, she had taken Tah and his older sister to live on the coast with her and their stepfather. Time passed, and Tah's sister mysteriously died. A brother was born, then another sister. Tah spent his days helping his family eke out an existence, leaving little time for school. The family's meager supply of money paid for the stepfather's drinking and gambling habits.

Then one day Tah's mother sent him to the market for a bottle of soy sauce. As he returned, Tah saw fire and smoke billowing out of the bamboo shack that had been his home. There had been a terrible explosion.

"Mother!" Tah cried in desperation as he ran toward his burning home. "Mother, where are you?" But she was gone, lost to the flames.

That night Tah huddled with his little brother and sister in the cold. No gentle arms held their shaking bodies. No soft hands wiped away their tears. They fell asleep, uncomforted and unsure of their future.

The next day the nightmare continued. Tah watched, heartbroken, as his stepfather first sold his brother to a Thai man and his sister to a barmaid from Kompong Som. Petrified at what would happen to him, Tah begged his stepfather to stop. But it was of no use. His stepfather sold him to a man from Phnom Penh. Crying, Tah realized that he and his siblings had been separated by a maniacal man who only wanted another drink. The price? Four dollars apiece.

And so Tah found himself on the streets of Phnom Penh without a friend in the world. But after the grandmother woman saved him from

Tah gives some neighborhood goats a friendly hug.

his slavery, he met the Griswolds, their student missionary, and an entire church full of loving people. Tah soaked it up.

He frequently came over to play with Joelle and to watch Nathan. He was fascinated with all the books in the Griswolds' home, and vowed that he would learn to read them someday.

"We have to get him into school," Julie urged her husband. "Let's talk with the principal of our new school here."

Within days Tah began attending the mission school, proudly sporting a new red-and-white uniform and showing off his Khmer alphabet to anyone who would look. Tah thrived in his new life. At church Scott heard him belting out off-key tunes at the top of his lungs. He was learning to love Jesus—and his broken heart was healing.

When the grandmother woman returned to the forest for more bark, Tah stayed in the city. He began boarding near school during the week and staying with the Griswolds on the weekends. The arrangement was perfect for everyone, and Tah continued to grow and learn in his friendly new environment. Time flew by, and Tah's first Christmas approached.

Scott jerked back to the present. Nathan had begun squirming in his arms, and Joelle was anxiously pounding on the window. "He's coming!" she shouted. "Let's show him his presents!"

Scott glanced out the window just in time to see Tah bound up the steps. "Merry Christmas!" Tah yelled as he flung open the door. To Scott's surprise, Tah didn't even notice his own presents. Instead he eagerly pulled out his gifts for Nathan and Joelle: tiny plastic fruits for Nathan and a motorcycle with a plastic rider for Joelle. "Do you like them?" he asked again and again, gazing happily at his small American friends and their new toys.

Scott stared at the scene in amazement. He knew that Tah had no money to buy gifts, but he had caught the spirit of Christmas anyway. The motorcycle was probably a toy he had just received at a school party. Suddenly Scott realized what he was seeing. Tah was pouring back out on others the love that he had received.

Perhaps this Christmas no orphan will come running up your steps. But down on the corner or across the apartment complex hall there are probably brokenhearted children who need your love. A boy who wants someone to make a snowman with him. A girl who's hungry for a Christmas cookie baking partner. Children who are aching for a Merry Christmas hug.

God gave His greatest gift. The Wise Men gave theirs. Tah gave his brand-new toy. What will *you* give this year?

1. Why do you think Tah enjoyed being with the Griswolds so much?
2. Why was Tah so excited about giving his presents to Nathan and Joelle?
3. How was Tah like the Wise Men in the Bible?

It's Christmas Eve. You smile as you glance around the family room. Almost every member of your family has come home for this important holiday, and you know that tomorrow will also be wonderful.

Suddenly a face pops into your mind. You remember Heidi, the strange girl in the grade below you, complaining that her Mom has to work all Christmas Day. "I'll be home all alone!" Heidi had whined on the bus just before Christmas vacation. "It's just not fair!"

Your conscience starts working on you, and you know that you should do something for Heidi. *How can you share some Christmas love with Heidi while still letting her keep her dignity?*

This Christmas or Christmas Eve, talk to your family about doing something for others. Go to a homeless shelter and distribute food. Instead of giving gifts to each other, give gifts to less fortunate people. Think of your own creative way to demonstrate your Christmas spirit to others in your community.

Together with your family, adopt an orphan from another country. It doesn't cost much to support one child, and your family can split the cost among yourselves.

Read and memorize Acts 20:35.

9

My Friendly Barber By Pearo Ackles

Pearo Ackles and his friendly barber

Pearo Ackles jumped as the stocky Cambodian standing beside him seized his head in a firm grip. Scenes of muscular Asians trained in martial arts and snapping the necks of their helpless victims came to Pearo's mind. He hoped his death would be quick and painless. A silent second passed as the barber savagely poised to wrench Pearo's life away.

Was this the result of some violent anti-American uprising? Were the upcoming elections in Cambodia somehow awakening deep-seated hatred? Or was it just a senseless act of brutality?

None of these appraisals were correct. Pearo was merely making his monthly visit to the friendly neighborhood barber, who had decided to help him get a kink out of his stiff neck!

Pearo's first journey to a Khmer barber was an adventure, as many mundane activities turn out to be in the mission field. The neck twist was not the only surprise. The menacing scissors flashed around Pearo's head and eyes, opening and closing rapidly. When they went up Pearo's nose to take care of business there, he wondered how many nasal passages these same scissors had already visited.

I really only need a haircut, he thought helplessly. He soon learned that in Cambodia a haircut is the cutting of hair, not only on the head and in the nose, but on the face. So even though Pearo had just shaved at home, the barber pulled out his long-handled straightedge razor.

I hope he likes foreigners! Pearo thought. He knew the razor could sever his jugular vein in a microsecond.

The barber silently affixed a new blade to the device, a welcome sight in a land of AIDS. The only lubrication utilized was a periodic splash of water.

The barber shaved Pearo's forehead, his temples, his ears, and the underside of his nose. The monks in Mongolia have their eyebrows shaved. Pearo prayed the barber would spare his. The barber attacked the area between Pearo's eyes and then the steely blade moved to his eyelids. The word "uncomfortable" does not adequately describe the unsettling experience of having one's eyelids shaved. Pearo did not move, flinch, twitch, or breathe. He quickly realized how difficult it was to keep his eyeballs absolutely motionless, but he tried nonetheless.

Christ's promise "You will keep in perfect peace him whose mind is steadfast, because he trusts in you" (Isaiah 26:3) came to Pearo's mind during this experience.

Since his first experience with the barber, he has returned countless times for more full-head haircuts. In fact, the last time Pearo went to the barbershop he nearly fell asleep!

Missionary life will always have surprises, for as it is for the Marines, "it's not just a job but an adventure." However, it surely is comforting to know that the Lord (and the barber) is on our side!

1. Why was Pearo scared of his barber to begin with? What kinds of preconceived ideas might have been in his mind about Cambodians?
2. How would you react in a strange country if something similar happened to you?
3. What special quality should a missionary have that will help him laugh about situations like this?

On a class trip to Washington, D.C., you get separated from your group. You're in a huge federal building, and before long you've gotten yourself completely lost.

Suddenly, out of nowhere, a tall man with arms as big around as your waist approaches you. Pictures flash through your mind of terrorists, bombers, or even assassins. The man smiles, flashing you a mouthful of gleaming white teeth, and points to his shiny security officer badge. He looks like Goliath to you, but you also know he's probably the man to help you.

What will you do?

Visit a church of a different denomination or ethnic focus to get an idea of how it would feel to be in another culture or country. Other ideas: Visit a cultural museum or event. Ask plenty of questions!

Get to know kids in your church, school, or neighborhood who are of a different ethnic background.

Many times people we don't understand will seem strange to us. If there are any "strange" or "weird" people whom you know, make it a point to be understanding. They'll probably turn out to be more "normal" than you think!

10

Children swimming in a Cambodian river

The God of the Rock

By Pearo Ackles

The scenic Tek Chou River suddenly came alive, but not with the swimming and splashing of the 500 vacationers gathered there. Instead, automatic machine-gun fire riddled the water's surface. Horrifying explosions of rockets and grenades now shattered the calm tranquillity of the site. A band of 30 heavily armed bandit-soldiers had come to rob and to kill. One hundred Seventh-day Adventist believers, the largest group at the beach that day, ran for cover with the rest of the frightened crowd.

"Follow me!" Pastor Lim yelled above the uproar. He ran toward shelter, followed by a large group of church members. Within seconds they were huddled behind a massive rock down by the river's edge. Explosions drowned out the cries of fear and pain from across the waterfront. Bullets screamed overhead, and leaves and limbs fell down upon the group of believers. The little ones did their best to stifle their cries.

"We're going to die!" August, Pastor Lim's bride of seven months, moaned the thought others were afraid to admit. Pastor Lim reached for her hand to comfort her. It was icy cold.

The brutal attack went on for more than an hour. It became difficult to decide which side of the rock to shelter behind, since bullets showered the area from three sides. But the group chose to stay by the rock.

After an agonizing eternity the thieves finally stopped firing. An eerie silence hung in the air.

"We know where you're hiding!" a voice called from beyond the rock. "And it's time to come out. Please step forward one by one, and we will relieve you of your valuable items. We will not hurt you if you comply."

Slowly, directed by a short man with a megaphone, the first survivors moved forward from the opposite side of the beach. Each individual was searched for jewelry, money, or other costly items, then sent back to their places. But miraculously, the man with the megaphone completely ignored the large group behind the rock.

At last the plunderers left with their stolen goods. The people on the beach remained where they were, too stunned—or too injured—to move. Pastor Lim, unhurt by any bullets, used the sudden peace to begin helping wounded survivors to the large mission van.

The soldiers had taken about 20 youths as hostages and porters and had killed an unknown number of others during the attack. Twelve church members were discovered to be missing, thought to be among those captured or dead.

"We've got to pray!" Pastor Lim encouraged the survivors. "It's not too late for a miracle!"

Although everyone knew that hostages were rarely seen again, God performed another miracle for the church members that day. Within several hours all 12 hostages were released unharmed and made their way safely home. And it was found that not a single Christian was even wounded! Soon, instead of weeping and shaking in fear, church members were praising God for His loving protection.

At a later celebration gathering, a young man read from Psalm 18: "I love you, O Lord, my strength. The Lord is my rock, my fortress and my deliverer; my God is my rock, in whom I take refuge. He is my shield and the horn of my salvation, my stronghold. I call to the Lord, who is worthy of praise, and *I am saved from my enemies*" (verses 1-3).

Get Into the Action!

1. Why do you think the thieves completely ignored the group of Adventists?
2. Why do you think no Christians were hurt in the shooting?
3. If several Christians had been injured that day, how could God still have used the incident as a chance to teach others about Him?
4. If you had been a surviving Christian during the attack, what would you have done for the survivors?

Scenario

You're riding the bus to school one day when some rowdy high school kids begin harassing everyone on the bus. Even the bus driver can't control them. They work their way toward the back of the bus, calling names and stealing lunches, lunch money, and entire backpacks from basically everyone.

For some strange reason, when the bullies get to your seat, they don't even give you a second glance! When the bus finally gets to school and the bullies run with their loot, most of the girls on board are in tears. You sit there, stunned that you have been spared. *What should you do?*

Take Action!

Read Isaiah 26:3, 4. There are countless people in the world who haven't found God's peace yet. Their lives are in complete shambles and they have no God to turn to. Watch the news tonight and find at least one person or group of people who could use some extra peace (refugees, victims of war, the family of a homicide victim, etc.). Create a care package to send to them. You might want to include things such as a devotional book, a family Bible you have highlighted and

The God of the Rock • Beyond the Edge

marked with special verses, several verses or encouraging quotes written out, a heartfelt letter, a tape of encouraging music, a book on how to cope with pain and loss, etc. If the people are from a foreign country, find a way to send them materials in their own language—or send something that anyone can understand (music, food, clothes, etc.).

Read Psalm 46. Memorize it and *use it* to encourage others. Volunteer to recite it at church. Visit a local nursing home or hospital, and recite it to residents and patients. Write it out and frame it for a friend. Be creative!

11

Sokhan

Sokhan sat in church, restless for the first time since he'd been baptized several months before. For a few seconds his mind focused first on Pastor Arnold Hooker, who stood up front delivering an emotional sermon. Pastor Arnold's face, already lighter than any other face in the church, shone with the same peace and joy Sokhan had finally discovered in Jesus.

Then Sokhan's thoughts turned to his mother. She lived in a village about an hour-and-a-half's drive from town, and ever since he could remember, she had been plagued by a demon. No trace of the peace in Pastor Arnold's face could be found in her permanently angry expression. "For the past 30 years," she was fond of complaining, "I have spent hundreds of dollars, going to witch doctors and trying to be cured!"

Sokhan squirmed uncomfortably in his seat, remembering the strange "cures" these doctors had prescribed. His mother had been told not to bathe for three months. She had been told never to comb her hair. For a long time, she was allowed to bathe only in urine. She even had been told to eat cockroach feces. She had faithfully tried all these things, hoping to appease the spirits, but none of them had worked.

"God has all power!" Pastor Arnold spoke from the front of the church. "If you ask anything in His name, He will hear you and answer you!"

Sokhan's heart beat faster and faster as the stirring words reached his soul. He had to tell his mother the good news! The minute church was out, Sokhan bolted for the door and headed for his mother's village.

"Mother, I am going to pray that my God will deliver you from the spirits!" he told her as soon as he walked inside her dark, tiny house.

She looked up, surprised and hopeful. Sokhan's faith was so great that he wasn't surprised at all when, after his prayer his mother leaped to her feet in joy. "I am cured!" she proclaimed. "I know the demon is gone!"

Sokhan was thrilled! His mother went up and down the streets, praising God and telling her neighbors about her miracle. She offered no objections when Sokhan told her to burn the small spirit house in her home, despite her neighbors' warnings that something terrible would happen to punish her. She knew she was freed!

Eventually, Sokhan went home and told Pastor Arnold and his wife, Stacy, about his mother's miracle. They, too, were overjoyed. But before long, Sokhan began hearing strange stories from his mother's village.

"The demon still comes," a visiting neighbor told him. "She has not been fully cured."

Sokhan immediately went to Pastor Arnold. "What did I do wrong?" he asked, his head hanging in grief. "I thought she was cured!"

"*You* didn't do anything wrong," Pastor Arnold comforted him. "Why don't you bring her here to Kompong Cham so you can teach her more about God? Don't give up! God is still powerful!"

Stacy agreed, and the next day, Sokhan traveled to his village to get his mother. They began studying together almost immediately, and his mother seemed receptive to the Bible. "I am so happy to be almost cured!" she would say over and over. One day, while Sokhan's mother and some other women were visiting a friend, Stacy came by to say hello. After several minutes she asked Sokhan's mother if she could pray for her.

"Of course!" she responded. "I would love that!"

She and the other women in the house gathered in a circle on their knees. All other sounds seemed to disappear as they prepared to talk with their Creator.

"Dear Jesus," Stacy began softly in a peace-filled voice. She got no further, because the mere mention of Jesus' name brought the demon back to Sokhan's mother. Several women screamed and cowered against the walls of the house. Sokhan's mother began rolling and crawling all over the floor and making strange noises. Stacy stared at her in shock. Was this the same polite woman who had been praising Jesus only minutes before? Stacy knew she had to do something.

"Ladies!" she called above the noise of Sokhan's mother. "We've got to pray! God is stronger than whatever force has entered our friend. Please!" She spread her hands in front of her. "Please pray!"

The women slowly quieted, and the hut filled with the sound of reverent prayers. Sokhan's mother seemed oblivious to their prayers at first, but after a few minutes she began to quiet down. Eventually, she stopped rolling around and sat still once again. Despite her disheveled hair and flushed face, it was apparent that the demon had left her body.

"Praise God!" Stacy said simply. "Thank You, Jesus, for saving Sokhan's mother."

"Thank You, Jesus." Sokhan's mother echoed quietly. "I know You have saved me for good."

After this incredible experience Stacy was a little afraid to have Sokhan's mother attend church. If just saying the name of Jesus made the spirit take possession of her body, what would happen at church? But Sokhan's mother truly believed that the demon had left her forever, and Stacy knew she should have more faith. Perhaps she really *was* cured.

Sokhan, his mother, and Stacy Hooker

The next week Sokhan's mother arrived more than an hour early for church, perched atop her spindly bicycle like a happy Cambodian bird. With a huge smile on her face, she told Stacy once again that the spirit had left her for good. And she was right. That day in church, Sokhan's mother sat fascinated with the sermon, the songs, and the stories. Never once did the demon enter her body. In fact, ever since the day the women prayed for her, the demon has not come back.

After several weeks, Sokhan's mother returned to her village. And for the first time in 30 years, her neighbors were pleased to see her. "You are so kind and loving!" they marveled. "What happened to the old, mean, cruel woman we used to know?"

Even the witch doctor was surprised. In all of his life he had never seen anything like it. "Will you teach me about this God?" he humbly asked Sokhan's mother. She could only smile in reply. She knew the God who had brought her this far had even more wonderful things planned for her future.

Get Into the Action!

1. How long had Sokhan's mother been plagued by a demon?
2. Read James 2:19. Why do you think the demon left Sokhan's mother's body when he prayed for her? Why did it leave for good when Stacy prayed for her?
3. Where do you think the demon went when it left Sokhan's mother?
4. Read Romans 8:38,39. How do you think God felt about Sokhan's mother during the time that she was plagued by the demon?

Your family has been praying that you will find a new house to move into for the past several months. In fact, it's been almost a year since your parents decided to move. There have been several good possibilities, but nothing has worked out. One day, you find your mom alone in her bedroom. You can tell she's been crying. When you ask her what's wrong, she tells you that she's beginning to wonder if God will ever answer her prayer. "I wonder if He even hears me!" She says to no one in particular. *You know you should answer. But what will you say?*

Believe that God is big enough to handle all of your problems! Re-read Romans 8:38-39 and rewrite it to fit your own life. What things seem to separate you from God and His love? Sin? Worries? Busyness at school? Write these things in place of Paul's list and save your version of the verses in a special place.

You may not know anyone who is actually demon-possessed, but Satan has plenty of other ways to torture people on Earth. Think of someone you know who is depressed, sick, sad, discouraged, or lonely. *Pray* for that person on your own. If you feel that the time is right, *visit* that person and pray together for God to heal and help them. Finally, *act* on your good intentions. Do what you can to alleviate the person's sadness or illness. Share Romans 8:38-39 with the person and invite them to rewrite it to fit their own situation. Be sure to show them the preceding verse, Romans 8:37, as well.

Adventist Frontier Missions is pioneering work in a closed country among an unreached people group in central Asia. For this reason all names from the closed country are pseudonyms.

 The names in this story are pseudonyms.

Nick wiped one damp palm on his leg and stared at his wristwatch for the fifth time in 10 minutes. He could feel perspiration forming on his forehead, and his sides were already soaked with sweat.

"Isn't that right, Nick, old pal?" Mark, his new friend from work, laughed loudly and punched Nick in the shoulder. "Women are all the same!"

A chorus of groans ascended from the women in the group gathered around the restaurant table. Nick's facial muscles twitched. Should he laugh or cry?

"Hey, let's get some more wine over here!" Mark called to a passing waitress. "Let the good times roll!"

No one at the noisy table that evening noticed how quiet Nick had become. He had barely touched his expensive plate of food and had completely refused any alcoholic drinks.

What have I done? Nick wondered as a wave of nausea swept over him. *How can I escape?*

He glanced at his watch. It was almost 7:00, and he still hadn't been able to get away.

Karl will start the Bible study without me, he realized helplessly. Every Monday evening Nick, Karl, and several other Christian friends gathered in secret and discussed the truths they'd been discovering. Every Monday, that is, until tonight.

Nick's thoughts retraced the events of the day. As a new teacher in the district he'd been dreading the day when he'd have to pay his dues. A cultural tradition stated that every new employee must treat his coworkers to a night of expensive dining. For the old Nick this would have been fine. He wanted to follow his society's customs, and he was a generous man, even though a typical feast could use up two weeks of his salary.

But several years ago he'd become convinced that he should follow the example of his new friend, Jesus. He had stopped drinking and smoking. His conscience had grown extremely sensitive, and he felt he simply couldn't pay for such a party. There would be drinking, after all. Lots of it. His new coworkers weren't interested in religion and took every opportunity to tell him dirty jokes and pressure him to smoke or drink with them.

But that afternoon he couldn't escape. It was a government holiday, and Mark had cornered him.

"Don't you owe us something?" he had asked Nick loudly, his eyes roaming the teachers' lounge for an accomplice.

Sam eagerly joined him. "Yeah, you do! When are you going to take us out? I'm free tonight; how about the rest of you?"

Despite his protests the other teachers had joined the plea. "Take us out tonight!" they had begged him again and again. Although each face had been wreathed in a smile, Nick had felt the pressure. *It's the rule in our society. You can't break the rules.* Defeated, he had agreed—and now here they were. The lights of the city's most expensive restaurant glinted off costly silver and spotless crystal while the talk around the table grew more and more unsuitable for Nick's strict tastes.

He cleared his throat. 7:05. The untouched white roll in front of him reminded him of something. What was it? *Bread. The Bread of Life. Jesus is the Bread of Life.*

That was enough. With a loud scrape Nick scooted his chair away from the table and mustered his most winning smile.

"Friends, it's been a pleasure. But I really do have to go."

"What's wrong? Have you had too much wine?" Mark shot back at him. Drunken laughter followed, and Nick heard several hushed whispers.

"What a sissy."

"He's not a real man."

"You know I didn't drink at all." Nick's voice was shaking. "And I'm telling the truth. I have an appointment, and I'm already late." That much at least was true.

"Who's it with?" Mark demanded. "Your mama?"

More laughter.

"No, it's . . ." Nick hesitated. "I have an appointment with the girl that I might marry." He said the words quickly, blushed a deep red, and ran from the restaurant amid the hoots and whistles of his so-called friends.

Nick ran all the way to Karl's house. When he finally arrived, huffing and flushed, he'd missed a half hour of Bible study.

"Something terrible has happened to me," he blurted out during the first lull in his friends' conversation. Then without waiting for their response, he rushed headlong into a description of the whole terrible day.

"And so I left them," he finally concluded, his eyes focused on the hardwood floor at his feet. "I ran like a lying coward. And I believe what they said about me. I'm not a real man." He waited for their tirade against his weakness and fear, but it never came.

Karl didn't speak. Gere and George, the other two men present, remained silent as well. Were they angry with him? Nick looked up slowly and saw tears glistening in Karl's deep-blue eyes.

Karl took a deep breath, placed a hand on Nick's knee, and bowed his head. He seemed to be praying silently. "Nick, you are not a failure," he told him simply. Karl reached for his well-worn Bible and opened it to a passage in the Old Testament.

"If my people, who are called by my name, will humble themselves . . . and turn from their wicked ways, then will I hear from heaven and will forgive their sin," he read quietly from 2 Chronicles 7:14.

"Nick, it's difficult to keep a strong faith when the devil pressures us from every side. But it's important to do what you have just done. You shared your struggle with us, your Christian friends. We can help you in your struggle. We can encourage you to turn to God in bad experiences." Karl's face brightened. "In fact, instead of listening to me tell you about it, why don't we all kneel and turn to God right now?" He smiled and slipped to the floor.

Gere, George, and Nick followed his example. As Nick began to pray, he realized with a start that this was a first for this tiny group. They'd never been drawn together in prayer until this moment.

Through my difficult experience, Nick thought to himself, *we've taken another step toward becoming brothers in faith. Toward becoming real men of God.*

Somehow the days ahead didn't seem quite as hopeless as they had a few minutes ago. He began his prayer with a smile of gratitude on his lips.

1. Why was it so difficult for Nick to leave the restaurant?
2. Read Matthew 10:28. How do you think this verse could be applied to Nick's situation?
3. How could Nick witness to his friends even after this embarrassing experience?
4. Should Nick talk to his coworkers and tell them where he really went that night? Why or why not?

Imagine that you are Nick—or Nicole—and you're still at the restaurant. Your heart is pounding like a drum in your ears. You know you want to leave, but you don't know how. If you tell them you want to go to a Bible study, you could get in big trouble—Bible studies are against the law here! On the other hand, they won't let you go without some kind of excuse.

Should you stay or go, and what should you do once you've made your decision?

Have you ever put a stop to some fun because you felt it was wrong? Have you ever walked out on a party or a group of friends? If so, think about the experience and thank God for His help in the situation. If not, imagine several scenarios that would make you uncomfortable, and visualize yourself asking God for help to make the right decisions. Imagine how you would leave (or stop) the situation and how your friends would respond. Be realistic! You may be able to use your ideas sooner than you think!

Read Matthew 7:1, 2. Are you, like Karl, the kind of person that friends can confide in without fear of judgment? Concentrate on listening to a person's story and responding in love instead of making a judgment on his or her character.

Pray for people anywhere who may be struggling with pressure to do wrong.

13

Paying the Full Price By True Andrews (pseudonym)

As True walked through the mass of people, donkey carts, and bicycles, he could hardly make any headway due to the press. Very slowly, he pushed his bicycle home from the Sunday market. Suddenly he felt a slight tug on his coat from behind. As he turned, he saw a familiar pair of honest eyes looking back at him.

True had first seen her earlier that day at the grain market, standing there with the best sack of yellow corn available. She appeared to be a poor peasant mother in her early 40's. *Here's someone I can do business with,* True thought. He knew that he would not only help her feed her family, but would also get a fair price.

After some bargaining, True and the woman had settled on 35 cents a pound, slightly above the going rate, but since the corn looked very fresh True was still satisfied. The sack weighed 75 pounds, and he hoped he could haul the awkward load safely home on his bike.

True reached into his pocket to pay the woman, but since he didn't know the local currency, he accidentally gave her 10 times too much. But the woman was honest and graciously gave True back the correct change. Grateful, yet slightly embarrassed with his fumble, True set off for home. *Cheryl will love this sack of fresh corn!* he thought as he pedaled, remembering her delicious stone-ground whole corn waffles.

He waited for the donkey cart drivers and tricycle cart peddlers to maneuver around each other. As he watched the traffic, he wondered how the truth could find its way into this incredible mass of people. He was sure that God knew each of them by name. How could he, one man, reach these people? The thought was deepened, knowing that for centuries these millions had faced a Christless grave.

True maneuvered into the street and was just about to pass a friend's rice and flower shop when he was surprised to see the corn sales lady again. In the 20 minutes since he'd bought the grain from her, he had traveled outside the grain bazaar and onto the main road out of the market. But there she was, holding some change in one hand, and holding the other hand out. She was obviously saying, "You didn't pay me all of what you owe!"

True couldn't understand the words she then said, and shrugged his shoulders. Could it be that he had given her less than what he owed? As he reached into his pocket to check, he realized they had better get out of the river of people before they were swept along down the street. They soon found themselves in his friend's rice and flower shop, and True hoped that his friend would defend him. He counted the remaining change in his wallet to be sure. Yes, according to the remaining change, he had paid her the full price for the corn. He tried to explain, but soon several onlookers became aware of the lady's charge against him and made an immediate jury decision: they were sure True was at fault.

True looked around. He was in a strange new country and had no idea what might happen next, so he wisely gave in to the building voices from every side that were shouting, "Ten more!" *Life is worth more than $1.22,* he decided, as he handed the woman more money.

But it wasn't the money that made True feel bad—it was the way he ended up looking. He had just paid a fair price at the bazaar, and now it looked like he, the rich foreigner, had tried to cheat a poor woman out of her needed income. That's bad in any culture! After she left, True tried once more to explain to his friend that he had indeed already paid her. But his friend only pointed to his head while shaking it, then pointed to True as if to say, "You are all mixed up. I feel sorry that we were friends."

How could such honest eyes be so malicious? True pondered this experience for a long time, wondering what he could have done differently. Displaying such large amounts of cash hadn't been very smart, he decided. The whole experience made it difficult to go back to the grain bazaar—or shopping anywhere else. True wrestled with his thoughts. *I really want to communicate love to these people, but so far it seems as if I can't even shop in a decent manner.* He tried to reason the best possible motives for the lady. Maybe she lost the money. Maybe her husband was upset that she had sold grain to a foreigner for such a fair price and she was apt to be in trouble with him. Perhaps the ends do indeed justify the means in this culture.

Even though True was still confused, he did begin to understand how God must feel toward the people in this closed country. God had paid in full the ultimate price for everyone's sins—His only begotten Son. But Satan has deceived this country's people into believing that God did not pay. Now they are very sure that God does not have a son. They don't know who Jesus is. They don't know Him whom God gave because of His immeasurable love. In the judgment they long to be represented, but they don't know who their mediator is.

True realized although Satan's deception looked like a wall, it could actually be turned around and used as an entering wedge because the people long to be represented when their cases will be decided. As he pedaled home, True hoped that people everywhere would pray that many would come to see the goodness of God in the price He has paid.

1. How do you think True felt when the woman asked him for more money?
2. What would you do if you were in a similar situation?
3. Why was it wiser for True to pay the extra money than continue arguing with the woman?

You're at a friend's birthday party, and a group of you decides to play a card game. You've barely begun, however, when Mark (the birthday boy) turns to you in anger. "You looked at my cards!" He yells. "That's how come you're doing so well in this game! You're a cheater!" The rest of your friends stare at you—they can't believe you'd do something like that. *How can you show your innocence while still keeping Mark as a friend?*

1. Sometimes unfair things happen to good people. Keep your eyes open for situations like this and make it a point to stand up for the person in trouble.
2. Read Proverbs 15:1, 18. Practice using "soft answers" when you get frustrated with your family or friends, and notice the difference it makes in your attitude and theirs.
3. What is the price for your sin? Read Romans 6:23. Who paid for your sins, and how do you know the price was paid in full? How can you show that you believe the price has been paid? Write down at least five ways to show your faith.

14

The names in this story are pseudonyms.

Amina's Star

Thirteen-year-old Amina lay down on her bed, her mind wrestling with difficult questions. *Who is God? What is He really like? Does He really care about me?*

Amina had always been taught that there was a God. Her father was a devout, religious person. But he was also a very controlling man and had practically forced her to follow his religious traditions and beliefs. Recently, however, Amina had been finding some other ideas about God.

Amina smiled, her dark eyes dancing, as she remembered the day when her foreign friend, Stacy, had come to her city. She couldn't believe that was almost a year ago. She and Stacy had quickly become best friends, talking first about "safe" topics and then about more serious subjects such as beliefs, religion, and God.

But that's where things had begun to go wrong. Her father hadn't objected to her friendship with Stacy until he found out that Stacy had been talking to Amina about religion. She clearly remembered the day her father confronted her.

"Are you a Christian?" her father had asked her just as she was finishing breakfast.

Amina hadn't known what to say. His dark eyes were on her, and she knew she couldn't lie. On the other hand, she already felt the rage he held against Christian believers. He would be furious to discover she believed in the Christian God. He might even beat her.

Amina had fiddled with her food for a few minutes before responding. Finally she came up with the perfect response. Taking a deep breath, she met his impatient glare. "What would you think if I was?"

"*Amina!*" His voice alone had felt like a beating. "You know exactly what I would think!" His shouts brought her mother from the next room. He was so angry by this time that he simply glared at her again without continuing the tongue-lashing.

Tears had stung Amina's eyes, but she knew she was safe for now. He hadn't forbade her friendship with Stacy!

Amina and Stacy continued to talk about religious things. Amina began asking serious questions about her beliefs, the Bible, and Jesus. She had been excited to discover that Jesus was powerful *and* kind—unlike her angry, cruel father.

Amina rolled over in bed. Tonight her mat seemed harder than usual. She thought of the doubts that had recently surfaced in her mind. Stacy's God had just seemed too good to be true.

"Are you sure He cares about me?" Amina had asked her friend that afternoon.

"Sure!" Stacy's laugh had bubbled from deep inside her, and Amina had felt a twinge of jealousy at her friend's easy security in Jesus. Then Stacy had grown serious. "Amina," she'd said slowly, "God cares about every person on earth. He cares about you. If you pray to Him, He will hear your prayer and answer it!"

Amina had gone home doubting, and now she lay on her bed, alone in her room. *Is it really true?* she thought to herself. *If God is so big, so great, so powerful, how can He care about somebody like me?* She heaved a frustrated sigh and slipped out of bed, anxious for a little fresh air.

Standing on the balcony of her bedroom, Amina breathed in

the crisp winter air. The coolness cleared her tired mind. Slowly Amina leaned over the railing to stare at the neighborhood below their fourth floor apartment. A few scattered lights shone through the winter night blackness. Not many people braved the chilly weather, and the silence was broken only by the occasional bark of a dog.

Next, Amina turned her gaze skyward. She scowled. *Just as I thought. Cloudy.* Even the sky seemed to mirror her mood that night.

Suddenly Amina had an idea.

"God," she prayed softly, "if You really exist and if You really care about me, let me see just one star."

She waited, looking up expectantly, but no star came into view. She stood there on the balcony for several minutes, her bare toes stinging in the cold, before retreating into the warmth of her bedroom. No star. Stacy had been wrong.

"You can't hear me, can You, God?" she whispered in the darkness. Tears threatened to spill from her brimming eyes as she fell asleep.

Several hours later she awoke with a start.

"Amina! Ah-mee-na!" Someone was calling to her from outside her room. But it was the middle of the night! Who could possibly want her at this time?

She threw on her coat and stumbled out to her balcony again, peering down into the darkness. Her eyes searched the street below, but she didn't see anyone.

"Who's there? " she called, but no one answered.

Confused, she searched in all directions, but still she couldn't see anyone. She was about to turn and go back into the house when she looked up into the sky. The clouds had parted, and in an instant she realized who had been calling her name. For there, above her, shining down its radiant light, was a single, bright, beautiful star.

1. Who do you think called Amina's name in the middle of the night?
2. What young boy in the Bible was also called in the night and reminded of God's presence in his life? See if you can find the story in the Old Testament.
3. Why do you think Amina's father was upset by her interest in Christianity?

You have recently made friends with a new kid at school. You've started eating your lunches together, and you discover that you have many similar interests. One day when you're listening to music in your bedroom together, your friend tells you that he is a Buddhist and wants to know what religion you are. Something tells you that there is an opportunity here, but you don't want to blow it.

What will you do?

Do you have any friends who don't know you're a Christian? Do you have any non-Christian friends? It's important to get out and tell others about Jesus—especially the ones who don't already know Him. This week, make a point of mentioning God in your conversation at least three times a day. Watch people's responses.

Read Colossians 3:17. One way to turn other people's attention to God is to give Him the glory for every good thing. Try turning people's praise away from you and toward God for the next several days. You'll probably get into more spiritual conversations than you have in a long time!

Have you, like Amina, ever wondered who God is? Have you had doubts about His presence or reality? Make a list of experiences (or reasons) that show you that God exists and that He loves you. Add to it whenever something new happens. In several months you'll have an incredible defense against doubts whenever they arise!

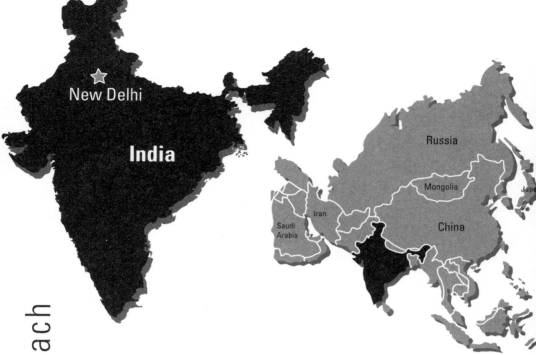

New Delhi

India

Russia

Mongolia

Japan

Iran

Saudi
Arabia

China

Specs: India is home to a billion people making up thousands of people groups. Most of these different people groups have different ethnic or racial backgrounds, follow different religions, or speak different languages. On top of these challenges, the caste system, a major part of Hinduism, still influences the lives of all Indians.

History: At one time, Christians were the fastest growing minority in India. This growth has slowed in many areas because of the reluctance of many new Indian Christians to witness. In many cases, churches are better at attracting members from other churches than winning over Hindus or Muslims. India gained its independence from Britain in 1947 and has fought 3 wars since then. Most recently there has been tension between India and its neighbor Pakistan

People: The Caste system is one of the biggest problems facing the people of India. Most of India's Christians are from lower caste origins and are still treated as "untouchables" by higher caste members. In many cities, idolatry runs rampant. Hindu temples are everywhere and people live in fear of their many gods.

A typical "holy man" in front of an Indian temple

DID YOU KNOW?

• India will become the most populated country in the world in the year 2020!

• India has more than 500,000 villages without a church.

• One out of every 4 blind people lives in India.

For a fee, oarsmen row people across the Ganges River.

15

Mrs. Silas and the Snake

By John and Beth Baxter

Mrs. Silas

John Baxter raised his hand to knock on the door. *Tap-tap-tap.* His knuckles created a hollow echo against the old wood.

"Just a minute!" Mrs. Silas's voice drifted out to John, her heavy Indian accent muffled by the wall between them.

As her footsteps drew nearer, John paused to thank his Creator for the Silas family. Mr. and Mrs. Silas had been the first Indian residents to encourage him and his wife, Beth, to come to Mirzapur. They had even opened their house as a temporary home when John and Beth had first moved to India. Now, months later, Mrs. Silas had agreed to study the Bible with them on a weekly basis.

"Hello!" Mrs. Silas's cheery welcome interrupted John's thoughts. She stood in the door, silhouetted against the white light behind her. A plump woman and the matron in her family, she carried herself with the pride of a queen. One expressive hand motioned John into the house.

"What can I do for you?" she asked as he entered.

John grinned. "You probably know why I'm here."

"I do?"

"I know why you're here," Mr. Silas said, looking up from his reading. "Why else would John come so late in the evening?" His wrinkled face broke into an unusually wide grin as he watched his wife's confusion.

John joined his friend's laughter, but his thoughts were swirling ahead. *Mr. Silas has been showing more interest in the Bible lately. Should I ask him to join us?*

John recalled the many theological discussions he'd had with Mr. Silas, each one ending without much change in his friend's religious interest. *I'd better not push him,* he concluded with a sigh.

He glanced at Mrs. Silas to see if she had remembered their appointment. Her eyes searched the room, John's face, and her husband's eyes for a clue to their secret. Suddenly light dawned, and she clapped her hands together in relief.

"It's Bible study night! I'm sorry I kept you waiting!" Mrs. Silas reached for her own worn Bible. "Let's go!"

Mr. Silas waved as his wife hurried John from the house.

"I don't want to miss any time with the Bible," she explained with a laugh. "Is Beth still awake?"

"Of course!" John held his flashlight as Mrs. Silas descended her front porch stairs. "She wouldn't miss these studies for the world."

"We're studying the last days again, aren't we?" Mrs. Silas asked.

"We sure are." John and Mrs. Silas walked across the street in silence. The darkness of the Indian night enveloped them, leaving only a pinprick of light from the beam of John's flashlight.

That's just how it is; isn't it, Father? John mused as he walked. *You have a few faithful lights in India, and Mrs. Silas is one of them.*

During the past few weeks John had been acutely aware of a spiritual struggle over the Silas household. He knew the devil wasn't happy about relinquishing his hold on Mrs. Silas and her family.

But if this means war, he reasoned to himself, *then so be it! God, You're far stronger than Satan!*

By now John and Mrs. Silas had reached the Baxters' house. "Watch your step," he cautioned as he stepped onto the dimly lit veranda. Hearing a sharp intake of breath behind him, he turned just in time to see Mrs. Silas's face contract into a mask of fear. In one sweeping motion she lifted her sandal-clad foot off the ground and spun in a complete circle. A startled cry escaped her lips.

"What? What is it?" John steadied her with one hand and pointed his flashlight to the ground with the other. Several feet away, a long, scaly reflection caught his eye as a quick and shining body slithered across the veranda.

Snake! The parallel fang marks on Mrs. Silas's foot confirmed their worst fears. She began to sob.

"Hold this!" John thrust his flashlight into Mrs. Silas's shaking hands. She obediently shone the flashlight directly at the snake's flat head. When it froze in mid-slither, captivated by the light, John immediately clubbed it to death with a piece of wood.

Mrs. Silas sank to the ground and began weeping uncontrollably. "It's poisonous," she sobbed loudly. "I'm going to die!"

Father, help me! John pleaded before speaking. "Mrs. Silas, you're not going to die!"

Beth, who had watched the commotion from a window, rushed outside with a charcoal poultice. "She's got to get to the hospital!" Beth whispered urgently.

John had already wheeled his bike to the veranda. "I'll take her right now. Please tell Mr. Silas what happened."

Beth nodded and reached down to help Mrs. Silas onto the bike behind John. In a moment they were off, careening through the narrow streets as Mrs. Silas wept. They arrived within minutes, but John knew that each minute counted.

The doctors immediately admitted Mrs. Silas. "The snake that bit you is very deadly," a white-coated man informed her with a sigh. "But we'll see what we can do."

Mrs. Silas lay back on her bed. "We can pray," she murmured softly. "We can pray."

The night dragged on. Crowds of family and friends arrived to comfort Mrs. Silas. Mr. Silas came, his usually jovial face dark with concern.

John prayed for Mrs. Silas. He read her the Bible and a portion of *The Great Controversy,* and anointed her head with oil.

"I feel much better," she assured him before he left. "I'm glad that silly snake couldn't stop us from studying the Bible!"

John laughed along with her, but his stomach churned with worry. He'd overheard a doctor's comment several minutes earlier—*"She won't live through the night."* He knew that Satan wanted to win the battle.

John and Beth awoke throughout the night to pray for their dear friend. When the first light of dawn crept into their bedroom window, John couldn't wait any longer. He dressed in a hurry and rode to the hospital once again.

"Is she all right?" he asked a frazzled-looking nurse near Mrs. Silas's door.

The nurse's face remained blank. "See for yourself."

Slowly, carefully, John pushed open the door. Would she recognize him? Was she in pain? How much longer did she have? But as the door swung open, he came face-to-face with a beaming Mrs. Silas! Her grin, which already looked as though it might crack her face, grew even wider.

"I wish you could see yourself now!" She laughed at John's surprise. "You look just like my doctor did when he visited me this morning. He told me I should be dead, but when he tested my blood for traces of venom, he couldn't find a thing! 'It's a miracle,' I told him. 'Praise God that I'm alive!'"

John sank into a nearby plastic chair. "H-h-how did this happen?" he asked in bewilderment. "How did—"

"*God* did it, don't you see?" Mrs. Silas was too excited to let him finish. "God saved me from the snake. God saved my life! I don't know how it happened, but I'm not going to argue!" She laughed again. "And I'm *definitely* going to be on time to our Bible study next week!"

1. How do you think this miracle might have affected Mr. Silas's interest in religious things?
2. Look up *presumption* in the dictionary. Would it have been faith or presumption for John to tell Mrs. Silas that she didn't need to go to the hospital, that God would take care of her without any medical treatment?
3. This incident happened while Mrs. Silas was in the process of translating *The Great Controversy* into the Indian language for her people. While Ellen White wrote *The Great Controversy,* she experienced severe illness. Why do you think both women endured such trials at those times?
4. How could the Baxters and Mrs. Silas use this experience as a witnessing tool at the hospital and among their other friends?

You and a group of friends are playing soccer during recess. Teresa runs to kick the ball into the goal, but the goalie is too fast for her. He leaps forward and kicks the ball as hard as he can. Unfortunately, Teresa is still in the way. The ball hits her face directly, smashing her glasses into tiny pieces. Teresa drops to the ground as blood appears all over her face.

What should you do?

Have miracles ever happened to you? to your family? List them all, and add new miracles to the list as you learn about them.

To add to your list, try getting stories from your friends or other members of your church. People love to tell their stories, and it gives them a chance to glorify God.

If there is no praise time during your church service, ask your pastor if you can start one. This would be an ideal time for your church members to share the miracles and blessings that have occurred during the week.

Learn basic first-aid skills, either by taking a class, reading, or talking with a qualified adult. Be prepared to help out in a medical crisis.

These men have been doused with colored water on Holi, *an Indian holiday.*

16

"Please don't go outside," Beth begged her husband, John. "You know what our neighbors said about this festival." She gestured out the window. "There's no telling what could happen to you today. Just stay home, John. Please?"

John stood with his hand on the door, unsure of what to do. He knew Beth was right. *Holi,* a Hindu festival deeply rooted in violent Indian myths, was a dangerous time to travel. Yesterday he had almost been hurt by a crowd of violent boys.

John glanced around his tiny home. Light filled every corner, and pictures of family members covered one wall. He *could* wait until tomorrow to visit the *Pratna Bhawan* (House of Prayer).

"I just don't know," he finally murmured, shaking his head. "Something keeps urging me to go. What if someone comes to pray and I'm not there?"

Beth sighed. "I suppose you should go."

John nodded and opened the door. "I'll be back soon. I promise."

As he stepped out into the noisy street, John hoped he would really be back soon. Memories of the night before troubled his mind. He'd been appalled at the violence of the people during this festival and afraid of the intoxicated crowds.

During *Holi* most young men painted their faces with silver and shot colored water at innocent passersby. They got drunk and danced wildly in the streets. Women prepared special pastries and drinks made from cannabis (marijuana).

Several weeks before *Holi,* firewood had begun accumulating on street corners and in public places. Last night revelers had ignited the hundreds of bonfires, and the young men had gone on a rampage. They climbed over fences and walls, grabbing whatever was available to put onto the fire. If anyone attempted to stop them, they were assaulted until they surrendered their rights and let the scavengers run rampant. The screaming and hollering had gone on all night, making it almost impossible for John or Beth to sleep. John had been grateful that he'd returned home before the fires were lit.

So why am I braving this madness again? he asked himself as he slid onto the seat of his rickety scooter. *Lord, protect me from the danger around me.*

The streets of Rupan, normally bustling with traffic, stood silent in the late morning sun as John passed through them on his scooter—silent except for a few raggedy gangs of young people roaming the streets in search of victims.

John made it halfway to the *Pratna Bhawan* before a group of boys spotted him. Liquid dye from bottles, tubes, and spray guns splashed against his skin and clothes, but John refused to stop. Suddenly a child leaped in front of John's scooter, poised to spray more dye at him.

John pulled hard on the brakes, barely missed the child, and crashed to the pavement with his scooter. Ignoring the child's cruel laughter, John eased back onto the scooter, determined to make it to the *Pratna Bhawan.*

When he finally arrived there, John's glasses were streaked with red and yellow dye. His clothes were ruined. And, to top it off, another crowd of vicious tormentors stood just outside the church.

"Get him!" they yelled as John dashed toward the building. "Get the foreigner!" Amid a hurricane of colored water, he yanked open the door and fell inside.

"Lord, why am I here?" John wondered out loud as dye-filled balloons spattered against the outer walls of the *Pratna Bhawan.* "No one will come to worship today!"

The Pratna Bhawan

Shaken, John knelt to pray. He desperately needed to talk with his Creator. "Oh, dear God," he began, "there must be at least 10 people here who will call upon You in love and truth. Will you spare the city for these 10? Call them, Lord. Please call them. Please forgive. Please remember your mercy. Please come quickly!" Hot tears rolled off John's cheeks. His head pounded with reverberations from the noise outside as it echoed in the church.

Slowly, as he waited alone in God's house, a calm entered John's heart. Even though no worshipers had come to the *Pratna Bhawan,* he knew that the people were watching him. He knew that they saw his devotion.

"Thank You, Lord, for bringing me here," John prayed again. *"Please protect me as I return home. I love You."*

When John opened the door of the building, the attacks began again. Several locals who had attended the *Pratna Bhawan* cautioned the crowd to leave him alone, but no one listened to them.

"Get the Christian!" they shouted again. A young man, his face painted beyond recognition, tried to grab John. But just in time, John jumped onto his scooter and sped away amid a storm of sticks and dye.

John careened through town, somehow avoiding the violent crowds who had chased him before. But just as he turned onto his own home street, he saw a menacing group of young men. He recognized most of them as neighbors and friends, but something in their stance told him not to go closer.

"Hi there," John spoke slowly. He hoped his voice wasn't shaking. "Can I please get through to my house?"

No one answered. The smell of alcohol hovered in the air like an angry fog. Suddenly one man reached for John's face, and another one lunged for the back of his scooter.

"No!" John yelled, blocking the chest of the man reaching for his face. But it was too late. A sharp yank from behind sent him sprawling on the ground. John leaped to his feet, looking for his attacker.

Smash! A wrenching pain in John's right arm caused him to stop. One young man, wearing a white T-shirt splotched with dye, had heaved a brick at him. Blood spilled from John's open wound. But he didn't have time to worry about it. Others in the group picked up rocks and hurled them in John's direction.

"Stop!" he yelled in vain. "Leave me alone!" John ducked behind a sign as the volley of debris continued. As he ventured back to his scooter, someone struck him along the spine and another kicked him in the ribs. When he confronted his assailants, the group swarmed him once again and began to beat him mercilessly. Finally a few rational men intervened, and John was able to escape. He stumbled into the house several minutes later.

"Are you all right?" Beth exclaimed when she saw him. Tears filled her eyes. "What happened to you?"

"I'm not exactly sure." John slid to the floor and held his arm. His head spun, and his muscles ached from the men's cruel beating. "Give me a minute to think."

He waited while Beth ran to get ointment and bandages. And strangely, the peace he'd felt at the *Pratna Bhawan* soon returned. A stillness filled John's mind. Slowly he began to sense his Father's presence.

Oh, John, My child, I wept today as I watched your pain. I love you so much that I endured beatings, spit, thorns, and ultimately the cross. I didn't deserve the pain either. But through all the mistreatment, I was silent. I looked at my executioners with pity, mercy, and love. I prayed what you must learn to pray.

John's body began to relax. He knew the prayer he should utter. Slowly, in the days that followed, he learned to mean the simple request. "Father, forgive them, for they know not what they do."

1. Why do you think the Indians were so eager to attack John?
2. Do you think John should have gone to the *Pratna Bhawan?* Why or why not?
3. Read 1 Peter 2:20-24 (especially verse 21). Did John do anything to deserve such treatment? How could he follow Christ's example?
4. Do you think the Indians would be impressed by John's consistent habit of going to the *Pratna Bhawan,* despite the danger?
5. Read John 15:18, 19. How could this verse comfort John after his experience?
6. Does the behavior of these natives mean all Indians would act the same way? Why, or why not?
7. Would you serve as a missionary in a country where these things could happen? What do you think Jesus would do?

Scenario

It's several years in the future, and the mayor in your town has issued a request for all churchgoers to stay home on Saturday because of the violent crowds who might harm them. It's Friday night, and you still haven't decided whether to go or not. *What should you do?*

Read 1 Timothy 4:12. You don't have to wait until you're an adult to have a good influence. Think of several ways that you can be an example to those around you, and try putting them into action.

Look up India on the Internet or in an encyclopedia. See if you can find any information about *Holi*. Ask your teacher if you can do a class project about Indian religious customs and holidays. Use this information to help you know how to pray for the people in India.

Read Isaiah 53. Make a list of all the descriptions Isaiah uses to prophesy about Jesus. From this list, draw a picture of Jesus, the example we should follow.

Read the story of the Crucifixion (found in Matthew 27, Mark 15, Luke 23, and John 19). Spend some time thinking and praying about what Jesus has done for you and how you can follow His example.

Rajesh at his baptism

At first Rajesh had just been curious about John, the white-skinned stranger who prayed at the *Pratna Bhawan* (House of Prayer) every day. Rajesh had politely taken the reading material John had offered, planning to throw it away. But once he began reading about Father God and Jesus, Rajesh couldn't stop! This was what he'd been searching for all his life! Alone in his bedroom Rajesh let the tears fall.

He was tired of his violent life. His father had been imprisoned for murder and other crimes until Rajesh was 9. His uncle had also spent many years in prison. His older brother had been murdered. And Rajesh himself had served time in prison for injuring an enemy in a fight. Now, at age 20, he was tired of the life he'd been leading.

Rajesh returned to the *Pratna Bhawan*. Week after week he climbed the sagging steps to the old church and joined John on the prayer mats inside. Slowly his heart began to change.

"I want to keep the Sabbath," he told John one

Rajesh By John Baxter

John Baxter and Rajesh

rainy day. "Does that mean I cannot work in the fields with my family on that day?"

Together they studied Exodus 20:8-11, and Rajesh knew what he must do. He thought about the money he earned each day in the fields. It was barely enough to survive on, but he knew that his Father God could take care of his needs. John sat beside him, waiting for a decision.

"I will not work this Sabbath," Rajesh decided without a second thought. "God deserves my complete loyalty."

Soon afterward Rajesh realized that he could no longer worship the idols in his family's home. When he made his decision public, his father was furious.

"You mock me by disobeying me! You must be punished!" he shouted at Rajesh as he raised his fists to beat him. Despite his bruises and cuts Rajesh stood firm in his decision.

"Get out of my house," his father ordered coldly. His dark eyes flashed with hatred. "You are no longer my son."

Fearing for his very life, Rajesh fled to John's home and stayed there for several weeks. Then John sent him to another city to receive more Bible training. While Rajesh was away, his father visited John.

"I am giving you my son. I don't want him anymore," he stated simply.

John didn't flinch. "Your son is a precious gift," he countered coolly. "I am giving him to Jesus Christ."

Although his father had stalked off in anger, something about the confrontation had soothed his ruffled feelings. When Rajesh returned from his Bible training, he was allowed to move home once again. Rajesh secretly praised God for this small miracle and continued studying his Bible in private.

One day an old friend walked by just as Rajesh opened his Bible.

"What are you reading?" the friend sneered. "More lies about Jesus? Give me that book!" In a flash he reached toward Rajesh, grabbed his precious Bible, and ripped a handful of pages from the middle.

"Give it back! That's *my* Bible!" As Rajesh reached for the Bible, his "friend" stepped away.

"That's *my* Bible!" the young man mimicked Rajesh. "You're such a baby." He spit on Rajesh's face, threw the Bible far away, and began attacking him mercilessly.

Rajesh felt hot anger rise in his throat. His violent instincts took over, and he lifted his sharp bamboo stick.

Thwack! Blood instantly appeared on his attacker's head. He fell to the ground and did not move. Rajesh stared in horror. *Love your enemies,* a small voice reminded him. *Do good to those who hate you.* Rajesh grabbed his Bible and ran.

When he arrived at the *Pratna Bhawan* that morning, Rajesh was trembling. "What should I do?" he asked John after telling him the awful story. "What if I killed him?"

In his heart Rajesh already knew the answer. *"Pray for your enemies,"* they had read from the Bible together. *"If someone strikes you on the left cheek, turn your right cheek as well."*

After some discussion Rajesh returned, apologized to his antagonist (who was in the hospital after receiving numerous stitches), and endured a beating as punishment for his actions.

"I have learned my lesson," Rajesh told John several weeks later. "I will never betray Father God again." He did not know how soon his promise would be tested.

Several days later Rajesh and his family attended a Hindu festival. When he refused to eat the *prasad* (food offered to idols), both his father and uncle beat him, causing him to flee for his life once again. A few days later his uncle and cousin met him on the road and tried to drag him into an alley to rough him up. The crowd that had gathered intervened, and Rajesh was able to slip away. He didn't return to his home.

Then one morning while he was out selling Christian books, his older brother stopped him in the street.

"Come quickly!" he panted, his eyes wild with panic. "Our father is very sick!"

Without a word Rajesh followed his brother home. But when he reached his village, he discovered that his father was fine and that it was a trap.

"Maybe a little solitude will clear your brain!" his father threatened just before locking him in a room.

And Rajesh had been there all day and all night without food and water. His empty stomach ached, and his tongue felt like a dry rag in his mouth. As the sun rose higher in the sky, the tiny room felt more and more like a baking oven. He felt as though he were one of his mother's clay pots sitting on the fire.

Will I ever escape? Rajesh wondered as he once again stared at the locked door. *Father God, Your will be done.*

"Rajesh!" A tiny voice interrupted his thoughts. "Are you alive?"

Rajesh started. "Little brother! Is that you?"

The door swung open. "Run! Do not come back!" His little brother, tears streaming down his face, handed Rajesh a drink of water and pushed him out the door.

Your will be done. Your will be done. Rajesh repeated this phrase again and again as he stumbled from his village for the last time. *Father God, You saved me,* he prayed as he ran. *I know You have a purpose for my life. Thank You for teaching me to serve You better. Your will be done.*

Postscript: *After a crowd of angry young men threatened to burn Rajesh and John Baxter for their faith, Rajesh decided to attend a two-year Bible school in a faraway place. John discovered that although* *most of the 50 Bible students he talked with could barely find different books of the Bible, Rajesh could name them in order backwards! None of the students had yet read the Bible all the way through—none except Rajesh, who has been a Christian six months. He is excited about his Father God and is eager to learn as much about Him as he can.*

Get Into the Action!

1. Why was Rajesh's family upset about his interest in Christianity?
2. Read Matthew 10:28. How does this verse relate to Rajesh's situation?
3. Why do you think Rajesh was so eager to learn about God?
4. How could Matthew 12:50 help with Rajesh's problems?

Scenario

Your family moves to a new town in the middle of the school year, and you enroll in public school. While most of the kids are nice and friendly to you, a small number of tormentors seek you out and make your life miserable. They taunt you every time you bow your head to pray at lunch. They make fun of you when you can't come to events on Sabbath.

You're at your wits' end! *How will you deal with them?*

Take Action!

Read the story of Daniel in the book of Daniel. What lessons can you learn from his faith?

Around the world, people are still being persecuted for their faith. Pray for these people tonight.

Make a point of being kind to everyone, even if their beliefs differ from yours.

Rajesh • Beyond the Edge

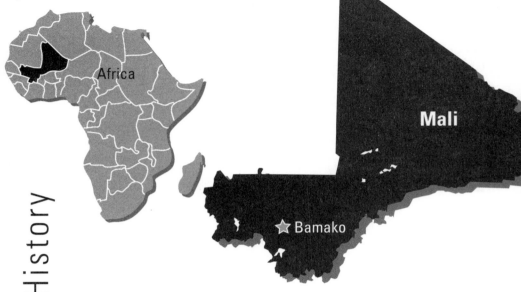

Mali: At the Crossroads of History

Specs: Mali, a landlocked West African country twice the size of Texas, has been at the crossroads of history for centuries. With Arab countries to the North and Black African countries to the South, Mali has grown culturally rich in music, dance, woodcarving, and other fine arts. The country covers three climate zones ranging from tropical temperatures in the south to an arid desert climate in the north. The combination of its location and climate variation has produced tremendous variety and a very self-sufficient Mali population.

History: In ancient times, caravans crisscrossed the land, carrying gold, ivory, and slaves for the north. Caravans headed for the south carried weapons, salt, and copper. Today, nomad people traveling in long caravans can still be seen outside cities like Timbuktu. France made Mali a colony around 100 years ago and French is still spoken today.

People: The country is split into two populations. The first represents agricultural people groups such as Bambara and Fulani. The second represents nomadic people groups like Tuareg and the Moors. One-half of the population is under the age of 15 and three-fourths live in rural areas. Since 99 percent of the country is either Muslim or Animist, many residents of Mali are still unreached.

Women in Mali pound their own rice.

DID YOU KNOW . . .

• Male members of the Fulani Tribe prepare for the courtship season by applying makeup to attract women of marrying age.

• It is incredibly rude to give or take anything in Mali with your left hand or to greet children!

• Be careful when you swim! *Bilharzia* (parasitic worms) are present in most standing or slow-moving water.

• When visiting Mali's capital Bamako, beware of determined purse-snatchers and pickpockets.

A Muslim priest and his helpers prepare a lamb for slaughter.

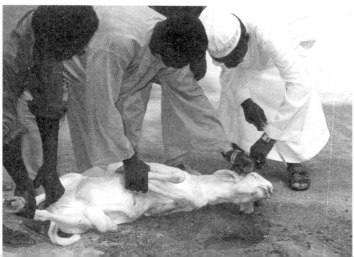

18

The Polley home

Bee Attack, Part 1 By David Polley, age 14

The Friday began like any other Friday. We went to the garden and back, ate breakfast, and started cleaning in preparation for the Sabbath. When I finished my chores, I remembered a bee tree my friend, Rashan, and his brother, Kareem, had found near their house. We agreed that one day we would go there and get some honey. We had suits to protect ourselves, and our parents said we could go if we were careful.

As I sat there thinking about that tree, I thought, *Today would be a good day to go.* So I got all the equipment together in a duffel bag and went up to Rashan's house. We decided to get dressed in our gear after we got to the tree so we wouldn't have to walk through the village looking like spacemen or something. On our way to the bee tree we passed some neighbors, who just laughed at us, trudging along with all our stuff.

When we got to the tree, we realized we had forgotten a ladder and something to smoke the bees out with. So we had to go all the way back home. On the way, we decided to scare Rashan's mom and sister by running around the house, acting like we were getting stung. It was funny when they really did get scared. When we started laughing, they knew we were joking.

We couldn't find a ladder, so we decided to get something to scoop the honey out with because the honeycomb was huge and hung low. We couldn't find anything to burn for smoke except some rubber, so that's what we took along. After making some adjustments to our "bee hats," we took off. I had no idea that this whole adventure of getting some honey would turn into one of my worst nightmares.

We left the house and went back to the tree. On the way we saw the neighbors again, and again they just laughed. When we got there, we were really excited and could hardly wait until we could get our hands on that sweet, delicious honey. I took the coals and the rubber and put them in a can. Using a long pole, I pushed the smoking can into the hole of the tree.

Now, some people say—and maybe it is even scientifically proven—that smoke makes bees settle down. But when I put that smoking rubber into that bee hole, within a couple seconds I felt something fall on me. When a bee lands on you, you usually don't feel it. So I thought that maybe honey was dripping, or that something from the tree had fallen on me. Then it happened again, and suddenly bees started pouring out of the hole like popcorn, thousands of supposedly smoke-calmed bees!

I yelled for Rashan to take the can from me (I was shaking in my boots), so I could get out of the bush that I was in.

Rashan shouted, "I think we had better get out of here!"

I was all for that! When I finally got out of the sticker bush and started moving away from the bee tree, the bees kept following us. Now I was really scared! We both agreed it would not be a good idea to go toward the village, because people would get stung. We had suits on and were not worried about ourselves, so we went toward our garden, away from town.

On our way to the garden we met a couple of girls. When they saw us, they ran as if they had seen a ghost. A little further down the road we heard a scream. I wondered, *Why would somebody be screaming?*

Then we saw people running from the bee tree. At that point I

A Malian tree

knew we were in a lot of trouble. Some men walked toward the tree, then a few minutes later we saw them running away and fanning the bees. About this time the neighbor woman came up to us, and she was not laughing any more. She was so angry she punched Rashan and snatched off his hat, which allowed bees to sting him several times in his head. She tried to punch me, too, but I was too quick for her, and we took off running again for the garden.

By the time we got to the garden, about a quarter of a mile from the tree, we noticed the bees were gone. So we decided to go back to Rashan's house to see if we could help anybody. On our way we met Rashan's sister, Sheneeka, running toward the house with bees all over her. As we ran to help her, I fell, and part of my head covering came off. I got up and kept running. When I reached her, she started to fall, and as she was falling she took the rest of my head covering off. From my left eye to my left ear, I got stung nine times, and once on my side. Rashan and I were finally able to help her into the house.

People began burning things to keep the bees away from the village. Rashan went back out to warn people and to let my parents know what had happened. Finally, my parents came on the moto (motorcycle) and transported some of the people back to our house. The rest of us grabbed lots of blankets and other coverings to wrap up in and walked through the village to our house. About 23 people were stung in the village. Our two families got the worst of it, including Mr. Martin and Joel, my brother, who were almost in shock from all the bee stings. (You'll hear Joel and Shaneeka's story in Part 2 of Bee Attack!) When we arrived at our house, we knew we'd been through the worst experience of our lives, and we thanked God that no one had been seriously hurt.

Next time, I think I will just buy my honey at the store!

Get Into the Action!

1. Why didn't David wait until his parents could help him get the honey from the tree?
2. Why did David and Rashan decide to go to the garden instead of running all the way through the village again?
3. Why was the neighbor lady mad at Rashan and David?

Scenario

Imagine you are in Mali with David and Rashan at the time of this story. Would you have gone with them to get the honey? Would you have done anything differently? *What kind of prayer would you have prayed when you were finally safe from the bees?*

Take Action!

1. Using a concordance, look up all the stories in the Bible that refer to bees.
2. What other dangers might a person encounter in Mali? Look up some scripture verses that could give the Polleys courage in light of these dangers.
3. Think of a time when you did something dangerous and God saved you from harm.
4. Thank Him for His protection.

Joel and David Polley

Bee Attack! Part 2 By Joel Polley (age 16) and Sheneka Martin

As David mentioned in Part 1, Friday began no different than our usual round of school, work, and preparation for the Sabbath hours. David and Rashan had come up with a scheme of getting honey out of a bee tree near the Martin's house. (The Martins live on the other side of Kangaba, near our garden.) I, being more cautious, told them they should really wait so we could try and capture the whole hive and raise them. We had received some bee equipment from one of our donors in Oregon, and David was so eager to try out this new equipment that he ignored my advice and decided to go to the tree.

I was cleaning the bathroom when David left to get Rashan for the expedition. At first I didn't know where he was going, so I didn't say anything to him. If I had, I could've reminded him to take the smokers that were under the bee suits in the storage room. As it turned out, using smoking rubber wasn't a good idea. Once I found out where he had gone, I quickly finished my chores, put on some pants and shoes, and decided to go see how they were going about getting this honey.

I was on my way out when Mr. Martin and Shaneka walked in. "I'm going to the carpenter's house in town," Mr. Martin told me. "I need a translator. Can you please come with me?"

I agreed, and we left about 10 minutes later. On the way to town, Shaneka decided to stay and visit a friend and have lunch. So I took the backpack she had been carrying, and Mr. Martin and I left. When we arrived at our destination, Brudilaye, the carpenter, had just finished eating, so we waited a few moments before discussing our business. After chatting for about half an hour, we headed up to the Martins' house. (I was hoping that David and Rashan had not finished getting the honey yet.)

It was a pleasant day, and we were walking at a good pace, talking about polygamy in Kangaba (Brudilaye has four wives). Once we came to the top of the hill, I could see a large Boabab tree about 100 yards in front of me. Not paying any attention to it, we took a right and walked along the road toward Mr. Martin's house. Of course, we were completely unaware that we were walking past the equivalent of a time bomb, ready to explode.

In the middle of our conversation, I casually looked behind me and noticed Mr. Martin swatting at something. Because flies are so prevalent in that area, I didn't pay any attention. But when the bug flew in my direction and stung me, I became a little worried but figured we had upset a small bee's nest and needed to move from the area. After halfheartedly jogging a few paces and noting that the number of bees was still increasing, I became worried and ran a little faster.

When we came to a fork in the road, Mr. Martin ran to the left, toward his home, but I kept going straight. Getting the bees off me was the only thing on my mind, not finding shelter. Realizing that running was not helping matters any, I understood why Mr. Martin had headed to his house. By this time we both had a huge swarm of furious bees around our heads. I turned and began running back toward the Martins' house.

I was really panicking by now. Stories of African killer bees leaving dead corpses for people to find in the middle of nowhere began running through my mind. All I could do was yell, "Save us, God!"

After running a good 300 yards, I was exhausted. (Never try running from a swarm of bees while wearing size 12 high-tops and baggy pants without a belt. It doesn't work too well.) As we neared the house the pain of all the stings was excruciating. Everything began to get foggy. I remember seeing Mrs. Martin running toward us both with a large towel after Mr. Martin and I yelled for help. Then I just blanked out. Shamarie, the Martins' other daughter, says that she saw me stop waving my arms and just stand there, sort of spaced out. She said I looked like I had an Afro (huge head of hair) of bees on my head. Mrs. Martin began to beat me with the towel, which I don't remember, and then she dragged me by the arm into the house. I came to again once I got inside and all the bees were off me.

We had made it! Truly, I was grateful to the great God of nature in having spared our lives. If we hadn't been so close to the Martins' house, we could have died from the stings. But the experience was far from over. We could still hear screams coming from the top of the hill where people were being attacked.

Then I remembered Shaneka. She had said she would come straight home after eating lunch. I silently prayed that someone had told her not to take the short cut from her friend's house, which ran within a stone's throw of the bee tree. A few moments later I heard familiar screams and saw two figures running down the same pathway we had left not 10 minutes before.

I'll let Shaneka tell the story from here.

My friend Fanta and I walked along, talking as best we can in spite of our language difference. Soon we were past the church and nearing the long space (about two football fields long) between the huge boabob tree and my house. As we walked along, a couple of really bothersome flies began pestering me. I hate flies. There are zillions here in Kangaba, and they all seem to love me, so I thoughtlessly fanned them away. But another soon joined the first two. They buzzed about my hand.

"Man, this is getting on my nerves!" I said out loud in English. Fanta said a few words I didn't understand (this happens a lot, so I didn't give it another thought) and looked a little worried. We both started to walk faster. The bugs followed and

Michael and Sharon Martin and children

seemed kind of mad for normal flies. *Come to think of it,* I realized, *they are really loud for flies!*

"*Lek se,*" Fanta repeated. This time she was a little more worried.

The number of bugs had tripled. As we broke into a slow jog, I smiled to myself. *We'll out run these suckers in no time!* And after a couple yards we did, so we slowed our pace. I turned and got one last glance at our unfriendly swarm. That's when I realized those bugs were *bees! Oh, well. They're gone now,* I thought. But as I turned around, I heard a loud buzzing sound and suddenly the air became thick as we hit a wall of live African bees! My heart froze. "Run!" I screamed wildly.

Fanta and I began to run as fast as we could, Fanta in the lead. I had on a skirt, sandals, and carried a huge backpack on my back. In my mind I kept wondering if I should stop and get it off. We were both being stung again and again, so I slowed down a little to try and undo the straps. Half running, I finally pulled it off. All I could think of was getting all those angry, stinging things off me!

Screaming for help, we ran to the neighbors, but as we neared the gate I saw that everything was closed up. No one was home! My heart sank as we ran toward the long path to my house. I felt so helpless. I was screaming, and trying to run was hard while holding my skirt and fighting bees at the same time. I could see my house now. It had never looked so far away! Then I took a closer look and saw that all the windows were closed there, too. We only leave the windows closed when no one's home, so I knew the door would be locked for sure.

Now I was positive that no one would hear our cries for help. Fanta was outrunning me, and I could see that a golden coat of bees covered her black hair. They covered our arms, legs, and faces.

I am going to die! They will come and find us dead along this path! I thought frantically. At this point breathing was becoming harder, and my screams become a faint call for help. *"O God . . . help me! Please . . . help me!"*

Our run was now becoming slower, and my whole body was in pain. Then I heard a loud voice shouting, "Run, run!" I was nearing the house. One of the windows opened a little, and I saw my family was inside.

"Run! Come in!" they shouted. But I was too tired, and I tripped and fell. Just then my brother, Rashan, and David Polley ran up. They knocked off some of the bees, and my brother half-dragged me around the house. My dad and Joel Polley stood on the porch, yelling for us to get in the house. They had their shirts off and were beating at the mounds of bees that clung to them

Once inside, I crashed to the floor. It was not until I changed my clothes that I got all the bees off. I could not believe I was still alive. We all had big cups of charcoal to take away the venom. I personally had had all the adventure I could take for one day, but I ended up going to the "hospital" here in Kangaba—a bee was stuck in my right ear. I am so thankful that I wasn't stung in my ear and that the doctor removed the bee with no trouble.

Although this Friday did not turn out to be what I had planned, I am so thankful to God for keeping us all safe.

1. Why didn't Fanta and Shaneka realize bees were attacking them at first?
2. Why did Mrs. Martin run to Mr. Martin and Joel with a large towel?
3. Why do you think the bees chased everyone and not just Rashan Martin and David Polley?
4. Why did Joel stop running when he had almost reached safety?

Your class has a pet snake in your classroom at school—and it's poisonous. However, Slinky has always stayed inside his glass cage and everyone has been safe. Until today. You come in from lunch early and find his cage completely empty! You know Slinky must be on the loose somewhere, and you feel yourself beginning to panic. *How will you safely alert your teacher and classmates—or the whole school—to the danger inside?*

1. Talk with an adult about what you would do in an emergency. Make a plan of action if there is a fire in your house, if someone gets badly injured at home, or if a natural disaster occurs (tornado, flood, etc.). Write out your plans, memorize them, and post them in a prominent spot in the house.
2. What did Peter pray when he tried (and failed) to walk on water? (Matthew 15:30) Remember this prayer the next time you are afraid.

20

Moumoumi's New Neighbors By Moumoumi

Moumoumi in front of his boutique

A number of months ago new neighbors moved in next door. When they first moved in, I greeted them. They smiled and nodded but didn't say anything. So I tried my limited French. Even in French, they couldn't get farther than the basic greeting and to tell me their names were Homer and Debbie Curry. Then they said, "That's all I know in French."

"What? White people who don't know French? Well, this is going to be interesting," I said to myself.

Before the Currys moved in they hosed down the entire house—ceiling, walls, floor, and courtyard. Wanting to be a good neighbor, I brought over a hose and helped. Though I might admit that the house was dirty, it wasn't *that* dirty. Soon after, they brought a ton of stuff to their new house. I mean, what more does a family need besides a few dishes, a charcoal burner, some mats, and, maybe, a few chairs?

Soon the Currys came over and asked if it would be OK to practice French with me. Then they said again, "That's all I know in French." They seemed to be saying this to a lot of people. Of course, I was happy to practice French with them. I wanted to be a good neighbor.

Over the months, I must admit that Homer and Debbie's French improved. They can speak about as well as I do now, though that's not saying a whole lot. If they would learn Bambara we could really communicate. They assure me they will begin Bambara soon.

One of the first things I noticed about this family is that I don't see them going to the mosque or praying at prayer times. Also, they didn't fast for Ramadan or sacrifice a sheep for *Tabaski* (religious holidays). However, they pray before eating. In fact, they assure me that they pray at least five times a day. And every Saturday morning I see them going up to the Adventist church. When I asked if they were Catholic, they said, "No." They don't pray with a rosary, and they don't eat pigs. I wonder what they believe about Allah? I have tried to ask them, but our communication was inadequate.

About the time the Curries arrived the people I was working for left, leaving me without a job. After a couple months, my friend, Moussa, asked Homer Curry if he would give me a loan to start up a business. Homer agreed to give me a loan, but there were quite a few rules. I had to get a quote on how much all the items would cost me, give him the selling price of the same items, I couldn't sell cigarettes, and I had to reimburse the Currys a set amount per day. They wanted to review the stock and finances periodically, and I had to bring them CFA5000 (US$7.50) before they would give me the money. I wondered why they wouldn't just give me the money so I could go to town, buy the stuff, and resell it. Why all the work? But I decided it was worth it. Now I've paid off the loan and have a thriving small business.

Sometimes Moussa and I take the Currys for a walk to show them around. Daoudabougou is a great place to live, and I like showing it off to them. Some of the sites of interest in Daoudabougou are the gardens, the river, and the houses made of *banco* (mud brick). Last year, we had an especially heavy rain and several *banco* houses fell down. One day we toured a mansion down by the river. Even the Currys were impressed by its size and the spectacular view of the

Moumoumi (standing), with the two Curry children and a friend

river from the house. What I'd really like to do is show them the cliffs and scenic beauty of my ancestral Dogon country. Maybe someday we can go there together.

Recently, I've noticed that the Currys have started sleeping outside under mosquito nets, just like I do. In this hot season it's way too warm inside the house. Many of us sleep on the rooftops or outside during this season. In fact, we were advised by the health officials here to sleep outdoors because the heat has caused some deaths, especially among children and elderly people.

I like when the Currys do things in a Malian way. Homer has a nice green robe with matching pants. Even their children, Jared and Caleb, have little green and purple robes. Debbie has a green and purple booboo and wears the head wrap with it. They look so much nicer when they dress this way. Sometimes Caleb rides on Debbie's back. It is a very natural way to carry children, and it keeps her hands free for other things. Debbie just had her hair braided into rows, like local women. *C'est très jolie!* (It is very pretty!) Now they're Malian!

The Currys tell me they will move to Kangaba soon. They are going to live among the Malinke people and learn their language. I wonder why the Malinke? Why not Dogon? I'll miss my strange neighbors. May the blessings of Allah be upon them.

1. Why didn't Moumoumi think the Currys new house was very dirty? What do you think the Currys thought?
2. Why do you think Moumoumi likes it when the Currys dress in traditional Malian clothes?
3. Why do you think the Currys are moving to Kangaba to work with the Malinke people instead of staying close to Moumoumi in his village?
4. Why is it important for the Currys to learn the language of the Malinke people, instead of speaking French all the time?

A new family is moving in next door, and you are awestruck. They look like they're from another planet! Their clothes, their accents, their manners—everything is completely different. You know they can't be from your country, and you assume they must be from far, far away. You notice that they have several kids about your age who look a little lonely in all the moving bustle. *How can you be a good neighbor to this new family?*

1. Prepare a welcome basket for the next person that moves into your neighborhood or joins your church. Include things like a map of the area, a homemade card, a list of all the fun things to do, your phone number and address, and some special Bible verses. Hand deliver the basket.
2. Make a list of things you can do to make new students at school feel welcome. Talk with your other friends from school and make a point of doing these things when new kids join your school.
3. Read Matthew 25:40 and 45. If Jesus moved in next door, what would you do for Him? Make a list of those things and consider doing some of them for the neighbors you have right now.

21

Close Encounter With the Dark Side

By Phillip and Naomi Polley

A Mali family altar

He's certainly a strange man," Phillip commented to his wife, Naomi, after their first encounter with Mr. Bala.

Naomi nodded vigorously. "I think so, too. But I can't pinpoint what makes him so strange!" She stared out the window after his retreating figure. "He speaks English very well, but that's to be expected from an English teacher. He was very helpful in translating for us just now." Naomi kept her eyes on Mr. Bala until he turned a corner and disappeared from view. "Of course, his clothes are a little wrinkled and his hair is quite messy for a teacher. But that shouldn't influence our opinion of him. What do you think?" Naomi turned again to her husband, who had been watching Mr. Bala as well.

"It might have had something to do with his laugh," Phillip suggested slowly. "Don't you think it was a little eerie? He kept bursting out with this odd laugh, even when nobody had said anything funny."

Naomi shrugged. "I didn't notice it. Maybe I was

out of the room when he did it. Besides, I don't remember anything funny being said during our conversation."

"That's just it." Phillip responded. "Nothing funny was said. Mr. Bala laughed for no reason. He didn't even sound amused!"

"What an odd man." Naomi shivered.

Phillip stood and stretched his lanky frame. "Well, let's wait to draw any conclusions. Maybe he's just got a unique sense of humor. Let's pay close attention next time we see him." He helped Naomi to her feet, and they continued their chores for the day in silence.

In the weeks that followed neither Naomi nor Phillip ran into Mr. Bala. He seemed to have dropped off the face of the earth, and the Polleys nearly forgot about their strange encounter. That is, until one sunny day when they decided to go for a walk.

"I need some exercise," Naomi announced at breakfast. "Kids, why don't you help me clean up the dishes so we can all take a stroll. I'd like you to meet a friendly woman I just met."

Before long Naomi and the children found themselves on a slender trail that wound through the tall grass. "I was walking yesterday," Naomi explained to them, "when I found this clean, neat house and well-behaved children playing out front. Their mother seemed so kind, I thought we should get to know her better. Here it is!" They rounded a curve in the trail, spotted the house—and came face to face with Mr. Bala!

He was sitting beneath a small, grass-roofed shade porch, smiling directly up at them. "My wife told me she met you yesterday," he said to Naomi in perfect English. "She liked you very much." Mr. Bala then let loose with his eerie laugh. Naomi glanced nervously at the children, but they had already introduced themselves to Mr. Bala's kids. She'd have to face him alone.

"Yes," Naomi answered stiffly. "I enjoyed our visit, too. I hope we can become better friends."

Mr. Bala laughed again. "I'm sure she'd like that."

An uncomfortable silence followed during which Naomi sought frantically for something to say. "How do you like your job as a teacher, Mr. Bala?" She finally asked.

Mr. Bala's smile broadened. "Oh, that's not my only job. I'm also the local medicine man."

"Oh, really?" Naomi's glance immediately shot upward to see if any strange items were suspended from the rafters of Mr. Bala's porch. She knew many villagers had experience with natural remedies for a variety of illnesses. She'd heard of a certain tea called *Kimkyliba* that was used for any stomach ailment, a tree whose bark could treat mouth sores, and a very bitter leaf used in the treatment of malaria. Seeing no such remedies hanging above her, Naomi stifled her disappointment and bade Mr. Bala goodbye. His other profession didn't pique her curiosity until several days later when she was on a walk with Phillip.

Once again Naomi found herself near Mr. Bala's compound. This time, when she spotted the strange man, she wasn't quite so nervous. "Phillip," she said proudly, after the usual five minutes of greetings, "Mr. Bala tells me he is a local medicine man."

"That's right." Mr. Bala laughed mirthlessly. "I have treated many sick people from this village."

Philip's ears perked up. "Medicine man, huh? I've always wanted to try some of the natural remedies in this area. Would you care to show me a few?"

Again, Mr. Bala laughed to himself. "I'm afraid I can't do that," he told Phillip calmly. "My knowledge is not in the area of natural remedies. It's traditional knowledge handed down to me from my father. With it, I have treated people from all over Africa, Europe, and even America." Mr. Bala paused to scratch the back of his left arm. "You see," he said slowly, "my father was an animist who kept—and prayed to—the fetishes."

Suddenly lights went off in Phillip and Naomi's heads. Mr. Bala didn't provide the same simple remedies they had heard about—he prescribed witchcraft! After their initial shock they were able to talk openly with Mr. Bala about his practices.

"I usually gather bark or leaves and use certain prayers to complete my secret prescriptions," he told them honestly. "I believe the only true religion in Africa is animism, or belief in the fetishes. Even if an African says he believes in one God only, he will always know that there is another god more powerful."

"Where do you think this power comes from?" Phillip asked him boldly. By now the three had taken seats under Mr. Bala's shade screen for comfort.

Mr. Bala looked away. "Some say it comes from Satan, others say it comes from God. All I know is that with a fetish you can do good to people, or you can do them harm."

Phillip sighed. Mr. Bala had evaded his question, but his beliefs were obvious anyway. He and Naomi left Mr. Bala's compound in a very sober mood. Mr. Bala's mention of "another god more powerful" had reminded them both of the voice of Satan.

"I know the devil wants to discourage us," Naomi said quietly. "But Mr. Bala is wrong about every African believing in animism, regardless of their other religions."

"That's for sure," Phillip responded. "I know many African Christians whose faith is stronger than the faith of some Western believers!"

Phillip and Naomi exchanged relieved smiles, but they both knew the reality of their situation. They were entering a place where another power was present—and they could be sure this dark power would be encountered again and again as they worked to dispel its effects among the people. Silently, they both prayed for themselves and for Mr. Bala, that the shackles that bound him would be broken, and he would some day proclaim the power of the true God.

1. What was so strange about Mr. Bala?
2. Do you think it was safe for Phillip and Naomi to talk with him? Why or why not?
3. How could they talk to Mr. Bala about their faith without making him angry or defensive?

"Let's see what's on TV." Jamie flicks on the television while you settle onto the couch. A mysterious-looking woman in a long black dress appears on the screen, advertising herself as a psychic who can read anyone's future.

"Let's try it!" Jamie suggests, already reaching for the phone. "Maybe she can help me know what to do about my brother. He says he's running away."

How will you respond?

1. Read Exodus 20:3. What things other than fetishes could become gods to you? How can you make sure that God remains first in your life? Pray that He will show you if you need to focus more on Him.
2. Pray for animists and spirit-worshipers in Africa and other countries.

119

Ulaanbaatar

Mongolia

Specs: Mongolia, one of the world's oldest countries, is known as a nation of nomads. Geographically, Mongolia is dominated in the south by the Gobi Desert, in its midsection by plateaus and steppes, in the north by high mountains. At one time, under Ghengis Khan, Mongolia became a world power controlling most of Asia in the 12th and 13th centuries. Today Mongolia is struggling to catch up with the rest of the world through modernization. The Christian church in Mongolia shows signs of rapid growth, but the majority of Mongolians still believe in Shamanism or Animism, fearing and appeasing the spirits.

People: While it's still possible to visit felt *yurts* (circular tents) and to see nomads dressed in traditional clothing, many nomads have settled down in large cities such as the capital Ulan Bator and have adopted more modern European styles. Many Mongolians still wait to hear the gospel in a country whose constitution guarantees religious freedom to all its citizens.

Food: Food shortages are a major problem, but there's usually plenty of mutton to eat. Dried cottage cheese, called *arul,* is eaten as well as *oroomog* or stuffed sheep intestines. Rice pudding, steamed noodles, stews, cabbage, and a variety of meat pancakes also make up the diet of a typical Mongolian.

Brad Jolly and a native woman stand behind a stack of special bread-like pastries. The higher the stack, the more mature the family who prepared them!

DID YOU KNOW?

• If you're offered a bowl of mare's milk, you should hold it with both hands and drink it all down.

• If you're invited into a *yurt,* don't sit with your feet pointed toward the fireplace.

• Everything closes down on Tuesdays in Mongolia.

• Because of Mongolia's climate, green vegetables are a rarity.

• Temperatures ranging from −54° F to 102° F have been recorded in Mongolia's capital!

These Mongolian children sport traditional costumes for the Mongolian New Year.

22

Pastor Bold

Bold's Journey By Cathie Jolly

So, what do you have to tell me?" The police officer's crisp voice forced Bold to meet his gaze.

Bold swallowed with difficulty and glanced at his friends. Sitting in a row in the police station lobby, they looked as uncomfortable as he felt.

Have they told him about our crimes? Bold wondered frantically. *I wish I could talk with them alone!* But the police officer hovered over them like a watchful mother hen.

"I know nothing," Bold eventually replied, searching his friends' faces for approval.

The officer slapped the wall with his massive hand. "Well, I see you will not talk in this room! Let's try another!" He grabbed Bold by the arm and led him to a nearby office.

"Sit," he commanded tersely. "Now, tell me. What do you know?"

"I . . . " Bold began to protest, but the burly officer cut him off.

"None of this fooling with me. Your friends have all

confessed. I know they've stolen many things. Besides," he sneered and his voice grew menacing, "if you don't talk, I promise I will put you in jail!"

Bold's heart froze. Jail? No! He had just begun to study and work toward college. And now, *jail?*

He sighed in defeat and leaned back in his seat. "All right, officer. I'll tell you everything."

Bold began with his teenage years, explaining that he had studied to be a Buddhist monk. He didn't mention that his father had died of lung cancer when Bold was only 14. He merely brought up his training to arouse the man's faith in him as an honest person.

"Unfortunately," Bold told the officer, "after I dropped out of high school, learned how to chant, and promised never to marry, I couldn't even join a monastery! The timing was wrong at each place I tried. My friends convinced me to change my mind about becoming a monk."

"Yes, yes." The officer nodded impatiently. "Tell me about your friends."

"They seemed to have a lot of money," Bold continued. "One day when I walked into my friend's house, there was a stack of money on his table. I asked him where he got it, and he told me that they stole some raw materials from people's yards. My friends asked me to join them so I could share the profits."

The officer grabbed a pen and began furiously scribbling notes on a piece of scratch paper. "Continue!" he barked after a short pause.

"Well, after five months of hanging around them, I felt guilty about what we were doing and thought that I should stop before I got into big trouble. I began attending high school and working. At my job they make me work very hard for very little pay, but I really enjoy the work." Bold sighed. "I haven't been in contact with my friends for several weeks. I promise."

But the officer didn't seem to hear. He leaped to his feet, grabbed Bold's arm again, and pulled him back out into the lobby.

"Well," he sneered in triumph, "I got your *friend* to confess." Bold's friends gasped and glared in his direction.

"Quiet!" the officer shouted. "I should have all of you sent to jail. But because of your friend's honesty, I'll fine you for theft instead."

Bold's friends groaned but eventually paid the money. When they were released from the police station, they turned on Bold in anger.

"Why did you tell?" they demanded. "We'll never trust you again!"

Bold felt terrible for betraying his friends, but even worse about his short career as a thief. His friends, unable to bear his higher morals, began to ignore him completely. With no social life to speak of, Bold spent his time studying to make up for the two years of high school he had spent at the monastery. One year later Bold enrolled in college.

"I've made some new friends," Bold's twin sister told him one day. "I've been attending meetings at Brad and Cathie Jolly's house. They're Christian Americans. And they're very nice!"

Bold stiffened. "Christians? Keep away from them!" He recalled the negative propaganda he'd seen about Christianity. "Our own religion is best! You know that."

Bold's sister said nothing more about Brad and Cathie, but she continued to attend their church. Several months later, while Bold labored over his impossibly hard English lesson, he remembered his sister's words.

"Hey!" he called to his sister. "Aren't your Christian friends Americans?"

"Yes," she replied from the other room. "And there's nothing wrong with attending their church!" Her voice grew louder as she walked toward his room. "Why do you ask?"

"I would like to go there this week to practice my English," Bold said simply. "These Americans could be very useful to me."

Bold had no idea that his life was about to change forever.

The first time he attended Brad and Cathie's church, Bold surprised himself by having a great time! The people sang and seemed to be having a lot of fun. Bold made more new friends than he'd hoped to meet all year. He was also laughing again— that's why he *really* liked the church. Back home, as he got ready

Pastor Bold and his girlfriend, Otgo

for bed, Bold wished that the next day could be another Sabbath.

Bold's interest in Christianity inevitably grew. He asked Brad and Cathie many questions and began searching seriously. After almost a month he decided that Christianity was something good and real. As a bonus he'd made so many friends that he felt as though he had a second family. Before long he was asked to help with parts of the church service.

I've been here for only a month, and I'm already teaching! Bold thought in surprise. But he enjoyed it so much that he wanted to teach more and more.

Today Bold has taken Brad Jolly's place as the pastor of the church in Mongolia. He explains his conversion this way: "I found that the explanations from the Bible were so real compared with the fairy tales the Buddhist monk told. God prepared me for this through my life experiences and lifted me up to the exact point of my greatest need. The time of my coming to church was the happiest in my life."

1. Why did Bold's friends get angry with him for telling the truth?
2. Why didn't Bold want his sister to attend Brad and Cathie's church?
3. If Bold had not received training to be a monk, do you think he would have accepted Jesus so soon? Why or why not?
4. What was Bold's favorite thing about the church when he first began attending?

"Can I go to church with you this week?" Sam, a friend from your neighborhood, asks you one summer afternoon. "It sounds like a lot of fun. And besides, I hear some pretty cute girls go to your church."

You giggle, but can't help agreeing. Of course Sam can come to church with you. Then you start thinking about what you've gotten yourself into. Will your church be friendly? Will Sam feel comfortable there? What if he doesn't like it?

Will you let Sam go with you to church or not? Why?

Take a look around your own church. Is this a place where you would feel comfortable if you were a guest? What would you change? What, realistically, *can* you change? Submit your ideas to the church board and see what happens.

If there is no "Welcome to Our Church" section on your church bulletin, ask your pastor or bulletin coordinator if they can put one in.

Look up Mongolia in the encyclopedia or on the Internet. Discover what the dominant religion is and what customs and culture Bold lives in. How can a person's culture affect his or her decisions?

Read Colossians 3:12-17. Memorize all or part of this passage, which defines a vibrant church community.

Nepal: A Tall Order

Specs: Landlocked between the two supergiants, China and India, Nepal rises higher than any other country on earth. Some have even called Nepal a blend of the best of India. Home to the famous Mount Everest, Nepal ranges from the growing modern city of Kathmandu to the mostly unreached people of the far west. Christian literature can now be freely printed and imported without restrictions, but religious and caste barriers still hinder the spread of Christianity to many people in Nepal.

People: The Nepalese people are very friendly. Newars, Indians, Tibetans, Limbus, and Sherpas are just a few of the people groups. Nepalese people are open to outsiders and their ideas, but seem to be very secure about the world and their place in it. Most of the people are either Muslim or Hindu. Among the Hindu, a complex caste system is still in place even though it's been illegal since 1963 in Nepal. This means that some Nepalese believe that they're born into "untouchable" families while others, such as the Brahmins, believe they're a "better" class of people. In fact, most Brahmins won't even eat the food that an untouchable has prepared.

The scenic Himalayas dominate the Northern horizon.

Food: In Nepal, the most common food is a spiced mixture of lentils and beans often served with curried potatoes. The Nepalese eat with the fingers of their right hand, as the left hand is not used for eating or shaking hands. Items should be given and accepted with both hands. It is very rude to offer a native of Nepal food that you have already tasted.

DID YOU KNOW?

• The monsoon season can leave mountain trails slippery with millions of leeches.

• Visitors should never wear leather clothing or shoes into Hindu temples or homes.

• Always walk around Stupas (a particular people group) clockwise and never step over any part of a person's body in Nepal.

• Nepalese dressed in all white should not be touched because they are in mourning.

Young girls often help their parents carry straw home from the fields.

23

Building a Christian Home By Rob Ernst

A typical rural Nepali house

Would you like to come visit my house?" Tage asked Rob Ernst one windy afternoon. "JoTee and I would love it if you stopped by. We'll even feed you a meal." His dark Nepali skin glistened in the sun.

Rob, who always wanted to get to know the Nepali people, agreed instantly. The two men set a time and parted ways.

Several days later Rob followed Tage toward a tiny bamboo hut built on government land. It stood alone on the patch of land, a curious contrast to most large Nepali family complexes. *I wonder why Tage and JoTee don't live near their families,* Rob thought as they neared the hut.

But before Rob had time to wonder any further, Tage pulled open the "door" to his hut—a rusty piece of tin hanging on several string hinges.

"Come in, come in!" JoTee, Tage's wife, called from somewhere in the darkness. "The meal is almost ready."

Rob ducked his head and stepped inside. The ceiling was no higher than his shoulders, and the hut look even smaller from the inside. A small oil lamp provided the only light in the room.

JoTee was kneeling on the mud floor next to the lamp, preparing the evening meal of rice and lentils. Rob watched her in silence as she held a pot of hot water over a blue kerosene flame. Her other arm cradled her infant son, Powell.

After a moment JoTee looked Rob's way, clasped her hands together at eye level as though she were praying, and said, *"Jay-riasee!* ["Praise the Lord!"]."

Recognizing the customary greeting of some Christian Nepalis, Rob cheerfully returned her greeting. *A Christian family in this unreached country!* He silently rejoiced. *Thank You, Jesus, for bringing me to this home today.*

"Have a seat," Tage invited Rob and gestured toward a small wooden bed. It creaked ominously as the two men lowered themselves onto it, and Rob couldn't help wondering how the family got any sleep at night. He spotted an old blanket rolled up at the end of the bed and realized that it was probably their only protection against the cold.

Just before the meal 18-month-old Powell crawled over to the bed and gazed intently at Rob. A yellow stream of pus trickled out of his left ear.

"What's wrong with him?" Rob asked JoTee in alarm.

"Oh, I'm not sure," she said with a sigh. "It's been that way for a week. We've prayed to Jesus and asked Him to heal Powell's ear, but He hasn't yet. We can't afford to buy any medicine. We even had to borrow food from our neighbors this week because there's no work."

JoTee turned back to her cooking, but Rob lifted his hand. "Wait! Let me show you how to clean his ear," he offered. Within a few minutes he taught JoTee how to clean the ear with some cotton and a matchstick. He promised to bring medicine for Powell as soon as possible.

"Thank you so much!" JoTee's face broke into a pleased smile of gratitude.

As Rob and the family sat down to eat, Tage began talking about his family.

"JoTee and I met three years ago in a Christian church in southern Nepal," he explained. "Both our families disowned us when we decided to follow Jesus. After we got married, we moved away because they caused so much trouble. They are still angry with us."

As Tage spoke, Rob glanced around the tiny hut. He noticed ragged plastic bags covering the thin bamboo roof and flapping in the wind. "Tell me about this home," Rob suggested.

"As you can see," Tage said briskly, "we have a very small home. We are poor. We don't have much money. I work whenever there's an opportunity, but that's not more than two or three days a week." Tage stared at the roof for a moment. "When it rains, what little we have gets wet. When it rains at night, it's especially difficult."

Rob imagined the tiny family shivering in the dark. "I have an idea," he said to Tage before leaving the hut. "Meet me in town tomorrow morning."

The next day he and Tage spent several hours selecting long sheets of tin at the local hardware store.

"What's this for?" JoTee asked the men as they unloaded the metal at their home.

"We're going to build a bigger house with a new roof!" Tage responded happily.

By nightfall the old house had been removed and a small new house had taken its place. As Tage, JoTee, and Rob talked together that night, the number of people sitting with them steadily increased. Finally, when the house was full, Tage turned to Rob and said, "Brother, we'd like you to preach the Word to us."

Rob was completely surprised but gladly accepted the opportunity to address the small group, most of whom were Hindus. Like the Bereans of the early church, they "received the message with great eagerness" (Acts 17:11).

That night, as he returned to his own warm home, Rob thanked God for the chance to minister to such a brave Christian family. He hoped that he and his family would be able to bring light to many more of the country's unreached people.

1. Why didn't Tage and JoTee have more money?
2. Why did they live so far from their families?
3. How else do you think Rob could make them feel included in the Christian family?

You're at a birthday party for one of your non-Christian friends. After the celebration and games, some kids are sitting in your friend's bedroom, waiting for their parents to come pick them up. Talk turns to religion, and you discover that you are the only Christian in the group.

"Tell us about your religion," someone pipes up. "What makes you a Christian?" A chorus of agreement ascends from the rest of the group, and you feel all eyes directed at you. *What will you say?*

Read and memorize Romans 1:16.

Read 2 Timothy 1:7-9. Make a list of the ways you can be bold for Jesus this week. Are there any situations where you are afraid to stand up for what you believe? Concentrate on being a stronger Christian (with God's help) this week.

Help out with a Habitat for Humanity project or another home-building organization.

Joyce Meyer with a woman whose baby she delivered.

24

The First Baby By Joyce Meyer

"Come quickly!" The messenger's voice held both fear and excitement. "Baby is coming!"

Joyce Meyer leaped to her feet. "We'll be right there!"

Joyce's heart pounded as she hurried to notify her sister Teresa. This was the moment they'd been waiting for—their first baby delivery in Nepal. The women grabbed the medical supplies they needed before rushing out the door.

"I'm glad this woman lives so close to us!" Teresa panted as they raced across a small temple courtyard and up a slope to the woman's house. The family's donkey, always present in their yard, snorted and brayed a few times before moving out of the women's way as they approached.

Teresa and Joyce quickly pushed their way into the front room of the house, which was also used as a store to supplement the family's income. Bags of potatoes, onions, noodles, and flour lined the walls, but the pregnant woman was nowhere to be seen. Finally an old grandma motioned toward the back of the house, and Teresa and Joyce hurried toward one of two small back doors. Opening it, they found the woman sitting alone in a small thatched-roof enclosure.

"This must be where she'll stay after the baby is born," Teresa whispered to her sister. Joyce nodded unhappily. She knew that Nepali women were considered unclean for 11 days after they gave birth and had to remain separated from all human contact during that time. Still, she found it hard to believe that this woman would be forced to live in such a small room.

Teresa, noting her disbelief, whispered another comment. "This is a deluxe room compared to the buffalo sheds most women have to stay in!"

Joyce gasped. "But it's so cold!"

The pregnant woman, who had been watching the sisters' exchange quietly, finally spoke. "We can ask my husband to sleep outside so I can sleep in the house."

"That's a good idea." Teresa smiled at her. "We should have talked to you first. Joyce, why don't you stay with her while I find her husband?" Teresa slipped out the door, leaving Joyce alone with the pregnant woman.

Despite the nearness of her delivery time, the woman's face betrayed no sign of worry or pain. *I shouldn't be surprised,* Joyce thought wryly. *She's already delivered four girls and one boy without my help!*

As she suspected, Joyce found the woman to be in wonderful condition. Her contractions were between five and ten minutes apart, and the baby's heartbeat was steady. "You could give birth very soon," Joyce told her seriously. "We'll stay with you until you deliver."

Just then Teresa returned with the good news that the woman could sleep in the house. Relieved, the sisters moved their patient

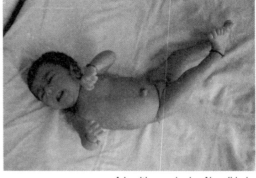

A healthy, squirming Nepali baby

Life for Nepali women is often very hard.

indoors. Still, the contractions had not sped up. Joyce became more and more sleepy as she waited, and finally she dozed off. Soon, however, the same anxious voice interrupted her dreams. "Baby is coming! Baby is coming!"

Joyce leaped to her feet and ran to assist Teresa, who had stayed with the pregnant woman. The mother was ready to push, and in a few minutes they witnessed the successful birth of a healthy baby boy.

"I'm so happy!" the mother said when her son had been cleaned and placed in her waiting arms. "Now I can stop having children! I have two sons. If something happens to one boy, there will still be one left."

Joyce and Teresa exchanged looks, well aware of the favored status of males in Nepali society. They knew that if the child had not been a boy, the mother might have held them responsible.

"We're happy too," Joyce finally answered. "You have six healthy children."

On the way back to their own house, Joyce and Teresa praised God for the safe delivery. "A birth here is so different from a birth in the United States," Teresa mused in the darkness. "Even hot water is a hard-earned luxury."

Joyce laughed quietly, remembering the small cup of warm water she'd been handed when she had really needed an entire kettleful. Somehow she had worked with what she had. Her face sobered as she remembered other events of the night. "They don't have towels, either. Did you notice that they wrapped the baby in old rags? It reminds me of Jesus' birth. And the cleanliness factor! Most of their babies don't even have diapers!"

Teresa sighed. "You're right. We have plenty of work to do here. But let's not get discouraged. After all, this is only the first of many deliveries!"

The two women spent the rest of the short walk home planning ways to improve the birthing conditions in their village. By the time they crawled into their own beds, their hearts were light with thoughts of healthy babies and well-cared-for mothers.

1. Why do you think boys are more valued than girls in Nepali society?
2. Why is hot water so hard to come by in Nepal? What might a person have to do in order to get any hot water?
3. Why do you think Nepali women have to be separated from human contact for 11 days after they deliver a baby?

Julie comes to school late on Tuesday, and soon the whole class knows why. "I have a baby sister!" she tells everyone who will listen. "Her name is Janie Marie, and she's beautiful! I got to hold her last night when she was born!"

Later, at lunch, you get to talk with Julie some more. "Yeah, we're all excited," she says, and then her smile fades. "All of us except my little brother. He's upset that Mom didn't have a boy for him to play with. You know, I think Dad's even a little frustrated—but he'd never tell Mom. I don't know what to do."

How can you answer Julie?

Visit a maternity ward and take congratulations cards to each of the new mothers. Ask the head nurse if there is any way you can volunteer in that ward.

Make a food basket to take to a local homeless shelter. Include things like toothpaste and razors along with the food.

Read Matthew 6:8. How has God supplied your needs in the recent past? What needs do you still have, and how do you know He will take care of them? How can you help someone else who is in need?

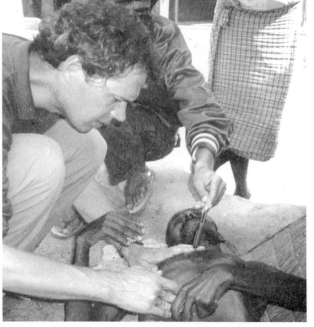

Tim Howe works on a Nepali patient.

Tim Howe, a temporary relief doctor for the Huwas medical clinic, glanced up from his work to see darkness settling over Huwas Valley. In the distance a dark silhouette waved at him and called his name. Tim grinned, recognizing the voice of his wife, Lynn.

"Supper's ready," she informed him when she finally reached the clinic. "Can you join us pretty soon?"

"Not quite yet. I have some work to finish up." Tim glanced at the sky, now completely dark. "Why don't you take my flashlight back with you? I'll come as soon as I can."

"But how will you get home without a light?"

"Don't worry. I'll be just fine," Tim promised airily.

Forty-five minutes later, as he waved goodbye to the last patient for the evening, Tim wasn't so confident. Although his family and his supper were a mere 50 yards down the mountain, the distance suddenly seemed endless. With a sigh Tim stepped out into the impenetrable darkness of a foggy, moonless night.

"I wonder where the terrace is," Tim mumbled as he

felt his way along the clinic wall. He shuddered as he imagined himself stepping over the sheer eight-foot terrace ledge between him and his home. Tim paused for a few minutes, trying to remember what his surroundings looked like in daylight. He knew a set of stairs made the terrace easy to navigate, but how could he find them?

"That's it!" Tim finally whispered. "There's a frangipani tree right beside the stairs. I'll just look for the tree."

Carefully, slowly, he began inching forward on the uneven ground. Within moments his hand brushed against rough bark.

Thank You, Jesus! Tim thought as he felt around the frangipani tree to the terrace ledge. He confidently lowered his left leg into what he expected to be a 10-inch step. But when his leg kept going farther down, Tim realized the truth: Any frangipani was not necessarily *the* frangipani he needed! He suddenly remembered seeing *two* large frangipani trees on the terrace edge.

Tim had no time to react. With a terrified yelp he landed on the hard ground eight feet below. Searing pain knifed through his right wrist, and he wondered how he would perform surgeries and medial examinations if his hand were encased in plaster.

"Lord, help me!" Tim groaned as he struggled to his feet. He remembered the villagers' stories of a hungry Bengal tiger that roamed this part of the valley. He didn't want to be its twenty-seventh victim. Spurred on by fear and pain, Tim wandered through the darkness until he finally found his home.

Why did You let this happen to me? Tim wondered as he tried to sleep that night. *How can I serve You if my wrist is broken?*

The next day, after a 12-mile hike to the nearest road and a two-hour bus ride to the nearest X-ray machine, Tim discovered that his suspicions were correct.

"It's broken," the doctor informed him, pointing to the thin fracture line on his bone. "I'll put a splint on it and let you go home, but be careful with that wrist. No more hiking at night!"

Tim nodded wryly. He waited while the doctor applied the splint, then broke the bad news to Ananta, his guide.

Ananta shook his head in sympathy, then gazed down the road. "We'd better catch a bus right away," he said briskly. "The doctor's right. You shouldn't be out late tonight."

During the bouncy bus ride, Tim argued with God. *Why? Why did this have to happen? You could have healed my wrist last night, or kept me from falling in the first place. What good can I do now?*

By the time he and Ananta got off the bus at the trailhead, Tim was exhausted. His wrist throbbed in pain, and he began to have doubts about hiking the four hours home.

Ananta instantly saw Tim's predicament. "I'll tell you what," he suggested. "Why don't we stay at my family's house tonight? It's only 15 minutes away." His brown eyes shone. "I know they'd love to meet you."

Upon Tim's agreement, the two men made the quick journey to Ananta's house. They arrived just in time for supper.

Ananta's family welcomed Tim with typical Nepali hospitality. They served him a supper of warm buffalo milk, rice, lentils, and a side dish of fiery-hot pickles. Dessert was fresh honeycomb.

"This is wonderful!" Tim enthused, enjoying every sweet bite. He was so famished after his long day of travel that he finished all the food on his plate.

"Are you still hungry?" Ananta's mother asked quickly.

Before Tim could reply she piled his plate high with a second helping of honeycomb. Tim accepted the delicacy, but after a few bites he noticed something strange. The honeycomb seemed chunkier than usual. In fact, it seemed . . . alive!

With a start Tim realized that the nutritive value of this treat was enhanced with tiny bee pupae. He hadn't seen them in the dim light of Ananta's hut, but they were unmistakable on his tongue! As he choked down the rest of the living honeycomb, Tim drew great comfort from the fact that he had asked God to bless the meal.

After his eventful supper Tim retired to the small sleeping loft where he was to spend the night. He was surprised when, one by one, each family member climbed up the ladder and squeezed into his room. Ananta arrived last, grinning sheepishly at his tired companion.

"My family has some questions about health," he explained. "Would you mind talking with them?"

"Not at all!"

Before long the questions turned to spiritual matters. Would only Christians be in heaven? Did Tim believe the world evolved? Was Creation reasonable? For two hours Tim answered the questions of Ananta's wonderful Brahmin family and prayed while Ananta translated. He began to see that Nepalis are deep thinkers, searching for truth in their world.

Later that night, after Ananta's family had asked all their questions, Tim lay on his sleeping mat, praying for each of them by name. He knew that although he would be returning to the United States in several months, he would continue to pray for this family. He also knew that God could use him despite his broken wrist. Suddenly he felt ashamed of his doubt and discouragement.

Thank You, Lord, Tim thought as he slipped into a deep and peaceful sleep. *Thank You for showing me that You can use me anyway.*

A Nepali "holy man"

1. What is a terrace and what is it used for?
2. What is a Brahmin? (You may have to look this up in an encyclopedia.)
3. Why did Tim feel useless after he broke his arm?

You and your family travel to Indonesia on a mission trip. You are overwhelmed by the new sights, smells, and sounds all around you—and eager to begin helping the Indonesians you've come to serve.

But before you get a chance to do anything at all, you catch a rare Indonesian sickness. You're weak and dehydrated, and you can't keep any solid food down. You realize that you'll be stuck in bed for the next two weeks while your family helps the people.

How can you be a witness in this situation?

List some of the limitations for service that you have encountered. (You're "too young," you don't have any money, etc.) Now list ways that these limitations can be turned into opportunities for service in other ways. Try these new kinds of service right away.

Pray for the people of Nepal, who have very few Christians to tell them about Jesus.

26

Tears of a Bride By Jenny Hargrove

Alisa Lorenz (left) and Jenny Hargrove after a hike through the mountains

Alisa Lorenz and Jenny Hargrove hiked around the last curve in the trail expecting to see a party, but nothing had prepared them for the size of this celebration.

"Wow!" Alisa breathed in awe. "This is going to be an amazing wedding ceremony!"

Jenny heartily agreed. The two student missionaries stared at the spellbinding scene before them. In the valley below, the people in a tiny Nepali village hurried along with preparations for the next day's wedding. Jenny and Alisa, who had hiked in to attend their friend Puspa's Hindu wedding, were eager to experience this new adventure.

The arrangements for the 17-year-old bride to marry the not-much-older groom had taken place between two wealthy families. From Puspa herself Alisa and Jenny learned that both families had spent a lavish amount of money to make the marriage memorable. Both Puspa and her husband-to-be belonged to the Neware caste, known for their extravagant weddings.

The minute Alisa and Jenny entered the village, the villagers caught them up in the whirlwind of last-minute preparations. Puspa was nowhere to be seen, so they watched and helped as busy workers set up huge tents for guests, hung lights and banners, and transplanted banana trees as fast as they could. Finally, when the sun sank behind the tree-covered hills, Tilok, Puspa's father, invited Alisa and Jenny to stay with his family. They eagerly agreed.

The next day dawned bright and early, and the festivities began shortly after sunrise. Since it was the Sabbath, Alisa and Jenny explained to the family that this was their holy day and that they must spend time worshiping their God. This was not offensive to the family in the least.

"The marriage ceremony won't start until sundown," Tilok told them solemnly. "We hope you will come back in time for that."

"We'll do our best," Alisa promised him quickly.

After sundown the two girls returned to find that the attendance had grown to several hundred people, all milling about, eating, and performing last-minute preparations—yet all expectantly waiting.

"What's going on?" Jenny asked an excited teenage boy.

He grinned and waved a skinny arm in the direction of the road. "We're waiting for the groom! He will come with a huge procession to the bride's house!" The boy disappeared into the crowd.

Alisa and Jenny spent the next several hours trying to decline the huge amount of food being served to them as the favored foreign guests. "No more!" they protested again and again. "We can eat no more!"

Finally sounds of dancing and music reached their ears. The crowd let out a cheer. The procession was approaching!

Jenny's heart beat faster as the noise increased. When the procession stepped into view, she immediately noticed a correlation to biblical weddings. Ten bright fluorescent lamps, mounted on huge batteries and balanced on the heads of 10 porters, loomed out of the darkness.

Incredible! she thought to herself with a meaningful glance at Alisa. *This is just like the story of the 10 bridesmaids in the Bible.*

A Nepali bride and groom

The procession drew nearer and flowed into the main street of town. Nepali fireworks exploded left and right. Several bands played at the same time, creating a cacophony of conflicting tunes. Finally a gaudily decorated car and a bus full of half-crazed relatives entered the scene. The groom and his family waited in their car until three male representatives of Puspa's family (all bearing torches) met them and welcomed them to the wedding.

The whole caravan halted as the representatives talked with the groom's family. Suddenly, prompted by some invisible cue, the rest of Puspa's family poured into the street from the house and tent on either side of the road. Cries of "Welcome, welcome!" filled the air. Children screamed in delight, and mothers forgot to shush them. Alisa and Jenny watched the whole scene in amazement.

In a series of rituals, pressing *tikas* (red powder and rice) on foreheads and offering the blessings of the spirits and gifts of worship to the groom, the group proceeded to the upper room of the house. There only the closest relatives (and Alisa and Jenny) crowded into the hot stuffy room and sat cross-legged on the floor. All eyes, which had been staring at the groom as he sat against the far wall, moved to Puspa as she entered the room.

Jenny gasped. She barely recognized her young friend! Decked out in the traditional red marriage sari, complete with gold trim, Puspa was heavily laden with golden bangles, necklaces, rings, and an ornate headpiece. She wore sheer red and gold cloth draped over her head to mask the half-drugged expression she wore. Weddings are a time of weeping for Nepali brides.

Immediately Jenny's heart went out to Puspa. The speedy arrangement of the marriage had been prompted by the fact that Puspa had had a boyfriend of a poorer, lower caste whom her father would not stand for.

Puspa's shaking hunched shoulders gave her away as she silently performed the motions of the customary rituals. The finalizing act of the marriage comes when the bride must bow and kiss the feet of her husband. At this point Puspa was sobbing so hard she had to be helped to her knees to reach the groom's feet.

The night wore on, but the highlight was over. Alisa and Jenny stumbled to bed, dazed and exhausted. The next day, as they hiked their way back through the mountains, Jenny thought of the life that lay ahead of Puspa. As was the custom, she would go with her husband to live in his house, where she would be a servant for her mother-in-law.

How hard life is for the Nepali people, Jenny mused as she walked. *I am sure God longs for them to know of His way, where all burdens and cares may be cast upon Him.* That day Jenny resolved to pray for the Spirit to move the hearts of the Nepali people so that their minds would open and their hearts would accept the way of the true and ever-loving God. *Then,* she thought to herself, *then they will be complete in a marriage with Him that will be the happiest of all.*

1. Why did Puspa get married in such a hurry?
2. Why was she so unhappy during the wedding?
3. How do you think the groom felt that day?
4. Why were Alisa and Jenny allowed into the most private part of the marriage ceremony?

"You actually hang out with *her?*" Jessica's voice barely hides her disgust. "What a nerd!" You must look confused, because Jessica continues. "I mean, look at her hair! It's so oily and stringy! And her clothes are always out of style. I'm sure she's completely weird, and I can't believe you let yourself be seen with her. Sunny is a completely off-limits person!"

You sit, stunned, as Jessica continues her tirade. You'd thought both Jessica and Sunny were pretty nice people. Now you're not so sure. *How will you respond to Jessica's comments?*

Are there any cliques in your school or community? Why are they there? What are the dividing lines between groups? Do you have friends in every group? Why or why not? Examine yourself to make sure you are an impartial friend to anyone who approaches you.

Make a point of smiling at several new people every day.

Visit a homeless shelter and work with the people for a while. Would it be possible to be friends with any of the people you meet? Why or why not?

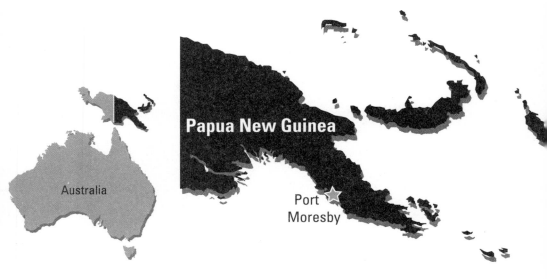

Specs: Not to be mistaken for Guinea in West Africa, Papua New Guinea occupies the eastern half of the second largest island in the world as well as several little islands to the north and east. The islands lay in the southeast Pacific Ocean near the Philippines. Considered to be ethnically and linguistically the world's most complex nation, Papua New Guinea's cultures have been formed by sorcery, fear, and warfare.

History: European explorers discovered the island in the 1500s, but it was left virtually untouched until the 1800s. During World War I and World War II ownership of the islands changed hands several times and over a million Americans fought on or near Papua New Guinea. The nation finally gained its independence in 1975. Today the residents of Papua New Guinea enjoy religious freedom. Many Christians participate in government and, due to the hard work of missionaries, nearly the whole country has moved toward Christian values.

People: Papua New Guinea contains about 1,000 people groups, speaking more than 700 different languages. The mountainous terrain is such that communities are isolated from each other. Most of the people groups like the Dowa fall into the major group called Papuans. Ethnic Papuans, who live mainly in the interior, are often physically characterized by other citizens as stocky and muscular. Dances celebrate everything from snakes to fire and whips.

Papua New Guinea

Natives enjoy eating grubs for any meal of the day.

DID YOU KNOW?

- Some residents ask for money if you want to take their picture.

- It's not customary to tip in Papua New Guinea.

- More varieties of orchids are found in Papua New Guinea than any other place on earth!

- In Madang fruit bats sometimes gather in such a large number that they turn the sky over town black. Bring your umbrella!

A closer look. Spit out the heads, please!

27

Alice and a little friend

Alice's Battle By Jeff Bishop

I can't find it, can you?"

Foggy voices blurred in and out of Alice's hearing. Her eyes searched the hospital room for her husband, her twin girls, *anyone* to give her support. But such a tight crowd of nurses hovered around her bed that she couldn't see anything else.

Alice leaned her head back on her pillow, lonely and afraid. None of the nurses could locate a vein so they could begin administering an IV. A curious needle had been pricking and poking her arm for the past 30 minutes. Alice wanted to scream at them to leave her alone, but she didn't even have the energy to do that. A single tear rolled down her dark brown cheek and onto the blanket tucked around her neck. Ever since she'd been diagnosed with severe asthma, her life had been turned upside-down.

As she silently wept, Alice let her mind wander back over the events of the past several months. It had all begun with her dream . . .

Alice and Rana strolled toward the tiny village in the

brilliant sun. Thick tendrils of smoke curled toward the sky from several cooking fires. The smell of roasting meat filled the air with a delicious . . . Wait a minute! The meat smelled awful!

"Go into the village," a voice commanded Alice. Wordlessly, she obeyed, gagging on the smell of cooking wallaby and pig meat. Alice left her friend and wandered through the village before meeting up with Rana on the other side. Suddenly the same voice spoke to her saying, "I want you to think about the meat you just saw."

Alice awoke with a start.

"What is it?" Her husband, Joseph, rolled over and stared at his wife in concern. "Are you all right?"

Still nauseated by the smell of the meat, Alice told Joseph about her strange dream. "You know," she observed several minutes later, "all the meat in my dream was meat that those Seventh-day Adventists don't eat. Why would I have a dream about them?"

But Joseph was already asleep. Alice stayed awake for several more hours, thinking. She had fought against the Adventists and their beliefs for years, and she wasn't about to change her mind now.

In the days that followed, Alice continued to eat her favorite foods: hot roasted pork and wallaby stew. However, she started getting sick after each meal. One day at the open-air market, she walked by a display of pig meat and nearly vomited. She had to cover her nose and run from the area. What was happening to her?

"Alice, why don't you serve meat at my meals anymore?" Joseph asked during supper a week later.

Alice nearly choked on her vegetables. "Don't! I can't even stand to talk about it!" she begged him. "I don't know why, but meat has started to make me sick!"

Alice, Joseph, and their twin girls were about to move, but before they left for Balimo, Alice had a chance to ask some of her Adventist friends about clean and unclean meats. "Maybe it's not such a bad idea after all," she reasoned to herself.

The move to Balimo was hard. Alice found herself alone again, struggling to make friends in the new neighborhood. One day while listening to her shortwave radio, Alice heard a man recommend a book that caught her attention. She wanted more than anything to get that book, but where could she find it?

A few days later Alice sat alone in her classroom, leaning her aching head on her hands. It had been a long day, and she wasn't looking forward to returning home and preparing a meal over a hot cooking fire. If only she had that book to read, she'd have something to look forward to at night!

Just then a tall White man passed Alice's classroom. His blue eyes caught her gaze as she stared out the open window. It was Jeff Bishop, the foreigner who lived in Balimo.

"Are you all right?" he asked her.

"I'm just thinking," Alice said with a sigh. "I wish . . ." Her voice trailed off, but on a whim, she decided to tell him. "I've been trying to find a certain book. I heard about it on the radio, but the only problem is that I can't remember its title!" Even Alice had to laugh at her predicament.

Jeff, who had stepped inside the classroom, sat down at one of the wooden desks. "That's a tough order." He thought for a minute, staring at his sunburned hands. "Is it *The Great Controversy?*"

Alice's head jerked up. "Yes, that's the one! How did you know?"

Jeff just smiled mysteriously. "I can get the book for you, no problem."

When the book arrived, Alice read it from cover to cover. She felt impressed by the material but hesitated to make a commitment to the Adventist Church, the Sabbath, or the loving God she was learning about.

Have I hesitated too long? Alice jerked back to the present as the needle jabbed her upper arm again. *Strange things have happened in these past few months. I can't eat "unclean" meat anymore, and I've had to accept the truth about the Sabbath.* Alice smiled as she thought of all the years she'd opposed the "seventh-day" people's strange ideas.

Lord, You win, she silently admitted. *You win and I surrender. From now on, I promise to keep Your Sabbath day holy.*

"I found it!" a nurse exclaimed above her. Finally the poking stopped and a cool, nourishing liquid began flowing through Alice's veins to the rest of her body. Smiling peacefully for the first time in years, Alice soon fell into a peaceful slumber. She knew God had won this battle, and she felt confident that He would continue to win all the battles in her life.

Within weeks all of Alice's family joined her in attending the local Adventist church on God's Sabbath day.

Get Into the Action!

1. How many different ways did God communicate with Alice about His desires for her life?
2. Why do you think it took her so long to respond to Him?
3. What radio program do you think Alice was listening to when she heard someone recommend *The Great Controversy?*
4. What other forms of outreach might touch villagers who otherwise would not listen to the truth?
5. Why might the Sabbath be hard for some people to accept?

Scenario

It's Sabbath afternoon, and you're lying around the house while your parents take a nap. When the phone rings, you jump for it and hope it didn't wake them up. Your friend Jesse is on the line.

"Hey," Jesse says, "want to meet me at the theater? My parents are out of town, and I'm totally bored. You can walk into town, watch a movie, and be home before your parents even miss you. What do you think?"

How will you answer Jesse?

Alice's Battle • Beyond the Edge

Start a new Sabbath tradition in your family by praying each Friday night at sundown for all the people who haven't heard about the Sabbath yet.

Read Psalm 19:1-4. According to the Bible, the sky is one of God's universal tools for reaching out to humans. Think of at least two different ways in which the sky could be a witness to those who have never heard of God. Now imagine that you are the first missionary to enter an unreached tribal village. You want to tell the people about God, but your Bible fell in the river several days ago. So you decide to turn to the sky—something everyone sees—and use the examples you thought of today. Write out what you would tell the villagers. (If you're feeling creative, make this imaginary story into a play for your church or Sabbath school class.)

Dale Goodsen and his guide, Yopa

28

Early one Sunday morning Dale Goodsen convinced his language helper, Yopa, to join him in an all-day hike. "I want to find the girl with the large tropical ulcer," he explained sheepishly. "She said she lived in Tapai."

Yopa grinned at him, his white teeth shining. "That's just an excuse to roam the bush, isn't it?"

Dale shrugged. "So I want to make friends. Is that all right?"

"Sure, sure," Yopa agreed. "You crazy missionaries always want more friends!"

The two of them started out, each carrying a pack of supplies and a few clothes. "We'll try to be back by nightfall," Dale told his wife, Lety, "but I'm not making any promises."

As it turned out, the extra provisions were a good idea. Dale and Yopa stopped so many times to bandage and treat sores that they made very slow progress. By late afternoon the two men were exhausted. They'd had only a few crackers and raisins for lunch.

When they came to a clear jungle stream, they felt more like sleeping by it than continuing on. But they gritted their teeth and pushed ahead.

At each village they came to, Dale and Yopa asked the same question. "Have you seen a little girl with a large sore? Where is Tapai?"

Unfortunately, there were so many girls with sores that the first question was more confusing than helpful. And asking for Tapai was not much better. They were first told that they *were* in Tapai, and then the villagers inevitably motioned down the trail and said that Tapai was *antop* (farther on).

"What's going on?" Dale wondered out loud. "Is Tapai just a myth?"

Yopa shrugged. "Just keep asking. Maybe you'll find out."

Finally a young man offered to take them to the place where the little girl was staying for a few days. "It's not far," he promised, then proceeded to lead them over rivers, across logs, down streambeds, and up dirt banks. When they finally arrived at the girl's village, the natives told Dale that she had just left for Kamina—a two-day walk from there!

It was late, and Dale was tired. He wiggled his toes in the cool streambed and stared at them incredulously. He wondered if he had sore feet for nothing. But the smiles of the people made it obvious that they were glad to see him and Yopa.

With a resigned sigh Dale went right to work. In a very short time he treated two older people with infected cuts on their heads, an old woman who had had diarrhea for a month, a boy with two tropical ulcers on one leg, a girl with more than a dozen infected sores on her legs, and many more sick villagers.

"We should go," Yopa finally suggested. "I need to get home."

Dale glanced at the sky. "You're right." The sun hung low above the treetops, and his shadow stretched across the entire village. Yopa found a papaya for supper, and they shared it before they left.

As they were heading back, it began to rain. Fortunately, they were just passing a large village, and one family invited them into their hut.

"Sure!" Dale agreed quickly. "I'm bushed!"

While the rain pattered on the thatched roof of their host's bush home, Dale explained his problems with finding Tapai.

"That's simple," the man explained with a laugh. *"Tapai* means 'place by a little water.' Every village is by a little water."

"So where's the *real* Tapai?" Dale persisted.

"Antop." The man shrugged and, like all the other villagers, motioned up the trail.

Knowing this conversation would get him nowhere, Dale asked if he could take a shower outside in a dark corner behind his hosts' home. They readily agreed, so he gathered soap and clean clothes, and stepped outside. The rain running off the roof would make a perfect shower.

Dale carefully stacked his clothes, then stepped into the cool stream of water. He grabbed some antibacterial soap and lathered up, but before he could rinse off, the rain slowed to a light drizzle. The few drops running off the roof were hardly sufficient for a good rinse. Dale's eyes began to burn from all the soap on his face, so he had to squeeze them tightly shut.

And then, to Dale's horror, a large pig emerged from somewhere in the darkness. His wild grunts spoke of unfriendly terms, and Dale was in no position to run!

Oh no! Dale thought frantically. *The last thing I want is to draw a crowd!* He knew that the people loved stories, and he had no intention of visiting their campfires and having all the kids request the story about the wild pig who chased the missionary while he washed and how the villagers saved the missionary just in time.

No solution presented itself, so Dale began a fervent prayer for help—his eyes were already conveniently shut, after all! He then waved his arms around and, hoping the pig understood English, whispered hoarsely, *"Go away!"*

After several more commands from the frantic missionary, the pig stopped somewhere close to Dale's feet. Dale was scared! He remembered stories of people who had been attacked by wild pigs, and a shiver raced up his spine. The pig's heavy breathing sounded deafeningly in his ears.

Finally, after a long period of tense silence, Dale tried to rinse his eyes and spread his arms to catch as many raindrops as he could. When he finally opened his eyes, the pig was gone! Dale wasted no time in drying, dressing, and jumping to safety in the elevated bush house.

As Dale lay down that night, itching from the dried soapsuds, he thought of all the events of the day: the miles of walking, the mosquitoes, his sore feet, the dozens of sores, the yards of dressings, the new faces and names, the invitations to come back, the language noted . . .

He was tired but content. *Someday these people will give their hearts to Christ!* Dale mused sleepily. *And whatever it costs—pig chases, long hikes, or strange adventures—it will be worth it to see these people in heaven.*

1. Why did Dale want to hike around the bush? Do you think this was a good way to get to know the natives?
2. Why was the village of Tapai so hard to find?
3. Why was Dale afraid of the wild pig?
4. Do you think Dale is able to laugh about this experience now? How would you feel in a situation like that?

You walk into the lunchroom at just the wrong moment. Lindsay, who is running with a tray loaded with food, suddenly slips on a patch of wet floor. Her feet skid forward and her tray flies backward, sending a shower of lasagna, milk, grape juice, and potatoes and gravy high into the air.

You duck, but it's too late. You slip on the same patch of floor, and before you have time to react, both of you are sprawled in a heap on the floor. The lunchroom erupts into laughter, and you feel your face turning as red as the tomato sauce all over your shirt.

How will you handle your embarrassment?

If you were placed in another country with a mission to teach the people there about Jesus, what would you do first? How would you help them trust you? How would you learn the language, and when would you talk to them about Jesus? Draw out a plan for reaching the people.

Fill in the following blanks: "You will be my witnesses in _____ (your hometown) and _____ (your home state), and to the ends of the earth" (Acts 1:8). Write out the verse, and frame it as a reminder of your responsibility to reach out to the people around you.

29

House on a Rock By Dale Goodsen

A typical house in Papua New Guinea

Dale rolled over and moaned in his sleep. A strange noise kept interrupting his dream. Someone outside was chopping wood—or was it a house being torn down?

"What's going on?" he asked Lety sleepily.

She sat up and strained her ears for a clue. "I don't know," she admitted. "Everybody should be asleep by now!"

"Well, I'm certainly not!" Dale remarked dryly. "I'll see what's happening." He slid out of bed, grabbed a flashlight, and followed the path to the heart of the village.

When Dale arrived at his friend Sod's house, a strange sight met his eyes. Sod, ax in hand, was violently demolishing his own hut!

Thwack! The ax struck a supporting post, and the whole hut quivered. *Thwack!* Sod struck it again, and the post collapsed. Most of the walls had already disappeared, and Sod showed no intention of stopping his attack.

No! Dale's mind screamed frantically. *Stop! You're*

destroying your home! You're destroying our Sabbath meeting place! They had scheduled church for tomorrow in this very hut. Dale longed to intervene, but the look on Sod's face warned him to stay back as bits and pieces of wood flew through the air.

I don't understand, Dale mused as he watched Sod chop away. *Sod his always been so calm!*

Recently Sod had chased a snooper from around the mission house. From that day on Sod had made nightly tours around the mission house to protect Dale and his family—"just in case." *So what's wrong now?* Dale wondered helplessly.

Sod stopped chopping for a moment and began yelling in the Dowa language, then went to the far corner of the house and knocked out the last remaining post in that section. Incredibly, the house remained standing!

Dale shuddered and began praying earnestly for the Holy Spirit to calm Sod down and to give him peace. *What should I do?* he asked God silently.

At that instant Sod stopped yelling and sat down for a brief moment. *Now!* the Spirit seemed to say.

Silently Dale walked back to his house and returned with a framing hammer, a pocketful of nails, and a flashlight. The air was tense, and Dale's every pore was conscious of Sod's sharp ax as he walked up to his friend.

"Sod," he began softly, "I'm concerned about your roof. It looks ready to fall down. I plan to quickly nail some posts back up before a wind comes." It seemed like a ridiculous thing to say. Dale felt like he was challenging a madman, but he hoped that this act of kindness would come as a welcome way out of Sod's anger.

Sod didn't answer, but his brooding eyes followed Dale around as he looked for usable supports and nailed them back to the most critical areas. With the help of a young man from the village, Dale soon had the hut in stable condition again. Even Sod joined in the cleanup of the scattered debris. Miraculously, the tension in the air disappeared.

His job done, Dale simply headed home. After a special

family prayer he toppled into bed for a short night's sleep.

The next morning the Dowa Adventist Church met, as planned, in Sod's barely standing home. The house was packed, and several people were obliged to sit under a neighbor's house to listen.

Dale said nothing more about Sod's strange midnight outburst, but he knew that it had to be Satan's effort to hinder the mission work in Papua New Guinea by destroying their meeting place. Thanks to the Holy Spirit, Satan had failed.

The newly reinforced house still stands, and the local interest in Jesus is stronger than ever.

1. Why was Sod chopping down his house in the middle of the night?
2. Why was Dale slightly afraid to approach Sod?
3. What was special about Sod's house, and why didn't Dale and Lety want Sod to chop it down?
4. How do you think Sod felt the next morning when he realized Dale had saved his home?

"I think you're awful!" Katie screams and grabs at a corner of your carefully typed science paper. Before you can stop her, she yanks the paper away and tears it into little bits. "That's what I think of you!" she yells as she throws the shredded paper back into your face. "And that's what I think of our friendship."

Katie stomps away, her back ramrod straight and her shoulders squared in anger. You stare after her in amazement. Yesterday you were best friends. What happened overnight to send her into such a fit?

How will you cope with this situation?

Read and memorize Proverbs 29:11.

Can you recall from the Bible a time that Jesus got angry? When is it all right to be angry, and what should you do with your anger? Make a list of the things you think it is all right to get angry about. Beside each reason for anger, suggest a possible way to deal with the anger. Pray over your ideas.

If you have wronged someone in your anger, ask their forgiveness.

Read 1 Corinthians 13, and make a list of all the ways a loving person should act.

30

The Yucky Lucky Lackey House By Holly Lackey

Heather Lackey

"I can't take this anymore," Holly Lackey mumbled under her breath as she swatted yet another mosquito from her bare white legs. "I just can't take it."

Thirteen-year-old Heather watched her mom in concern. "Are you OK?" she finally asked, afraid to disrupt the thundercloud that seemed to be hanging over her mother's head lately.

"Yes." Holly forced a smile and bent over a huge pile of supplies to hide her tears. *No,* she screamed inside. *No, I am not OK.*

As she sorted through the pile in search of the family's mosquito nets, Holly's thoughts trailed over the past several weeks. They'd traveled to May River expecting the worst—and now it had finally happened! After a few weeks of sojourn in the Kents' comfortable home, they had to move. The Kents were returning from furlough tomorrow and needed their house for their own large family. Like it or not, the Lackeys were stuck with the Yucky House.

Sure, Holly mused as she yanked first one, then

another mosquito net from under a sack of rice, *the kids and I could have traveled back to Wewak to wait for David to finish his business here.* But nobody had wanted to be separated from Dad for that long. So here they were, on their first night in the Yucky House, together but miserable in the rundown abode.

Exactly how bad was it? Once used by the government, the shack now lay abandoned and full of debris. A strange smell wafted from several unidentifiable heaps of rubbish, probably leftovers from the home's last occupants. Although the whole family had worked doggedly for several days, cleaning and making needed repairs, the house still needed help.

Holly yanked the last of the mosquito nets out of the pile and draped it over Heather's bed. "This will have to do," she sighed to herself. *Yes,* a small voice inside her responded, *it will have to do. Stop complaining! At least you have a home!*

Ashamed, Holly forced another smile and went to help David light the stubborn lantern.

Somehow the Lackeys survived their first night in the Yucky House and set to work to improve their situation. They patched the biggest holes in the walls, covered the slats on the floor, waged war on the rats, mosquitoes, ants, and various other creatures that didn't want to leave, and eventually installed an outhouse and an outdoor sink with running water. But Holly still had her "down days."

One morning she woke up determined to have a good attitude—and promptly found a new dress her sister had sent her lying in the mud. With an anguished cry Holly ran to rescue it, but it was too late. It had blown off the clothesline during the night and was now a muddy mess instead of the crisp white dress of the day before. As she scrubbed the dress with limited success, Holly thought about all the conveniences she had left behind. Just as a torrent of hot, bitter tears began to course down her face, someone called her name.

"Holly! Hollllyyy!"

Wiping her eyes, Holly turned to smile at a stoop-shouldered old man grinning at her from the trail. "I'm on my way to the clinic," he told her sheepishly. "And this bag of food is so heavy.

Holly Lackey

Can I leave it here at the bottom of the hill until I return?"

Holly nodded mechanically, but the old man didn't leave. Shyly he pointed to the Kents' dog, who was lying on the porch, and said, *"No gut dok I kai kai* ["That no good dog he eats."]." Holly understood. He didn't want the dog to eat his precious food while he was gone.

Holly helped the man set his food inside the door of the house, then watched as he struggled up the hill. And again she began to cry. *Here I am, worrying about a spoiled dress when this man has to worry about something as basic as his next meal,* she scolded herself. *I've got to refocus.*

After a long walk and talk with God, Holly returned to the Yucky House to find two notes that Heather had written on nice stationery, rolled up, and tied with some pretty embroidery floss. On the first were the words, "Turn your eyes upon Jesus, look full in His wonderful face; and the things of earth will grow strangely dim in the light of His glory and grace."

On the second Holly found the words of Jesus from Mark 10:29, 30. "No one who has left home or brothers or sisters or mother or father or children or fields for me and the gospel will fail to receive a hundred times as much in this present age . . . and in the age to come, eternal life."

For the third time that day hot tears welled in Holly's eyes and she cried. But this time it was a good cry. She saw the blessings she'd been blind to before. Her family was in good health and together, and they had the peace and joy of being where the Lord wanted them to be, doing what He had given them to do.

Slowly, over the next several months, the Yucky House began to look more like a home. In time someone renamed it "The Yucky Lucky Lackey House."

1. What things frustrated Holly about her life in Papua New Guinea?
2. How did Holly's daughter, Heather, help her out?
3. How did the old man Holly encountered remind her of her blessings?
4. How might Romans 8:18 be a comfort to Holly?

Scenario

You kick the door to your room shut and without bothering to turn on the light, flop onto the floor by your bed. It's been another rotten day at school, and you came home to find your parents poring over the checkbook, worrying about money. You don't want to tell them that you need $25 to go on the next school field trip, but you have to have the money by tomorrow.

Tears threaten to overtake you, and you try to brush them away. You've never been this depressed in your life! You feel like sleeping for the next three weeks without waking up. *How can you begin to cure your depression?*

When a new kid moves into your neighborhood or begins attending church or school with you, be the first to welcome them. Make sure they know their way around, and contact them at least once a week just to see how they're doing. You'd be surprised at the difference one friend can make in another person's life.

Try to remember a terrible day you have had lately. Think of some positive things that happened in the same day. How could you have focused on your blessings instead of your trials? How can you put this insight to use in the future?

Read and memorize Philippians 4:8. Write down the adjectives listed in the verse, and place it on your mirror or in a school notebook to remind you to think about good things.

Rachel and friends

(Jeff Bishop wrote this letter just before saying goodbye to his daughter after furlough. Rachel stayed in the United States to finish her last two years of high school.)

Dear Rachel/Tagiyato,

I just wanted to take a few minutes to tell the world what a difference you have made in the lives of the Gogodala people. You were only 12 when you arrived on PNG soil back in 1997, and had your first birthday overseas just one month later. Thirteen! Finally a teenager, yet stuck in the middle of nowhere, with no phone, no malls, no friends, and no junk food. Instead of a classroom of friends, you had only Dad and Mom as your teachers as you finished your seventh and eighth grade schoolwork. But a new curriculum was just opening up for you. An education you can't get in America. Four months later, when we moved to the village and into a bush house, each new day greeted you with a dead rat or two at your pillow, courtesy of your cat. Yet, you maintained a cheerful and adventurous attitude.

I remember you helping people with their medical problems, treating malaria and pneumonia and bandaging sores, even when the patient had to look real hard to find a sore just so they could have this new *tobadanapa* (White girl) take care of them. And then there was your confusion with the language. No, not Gogodala—English. Like the time when you asked to use someone's "bathroom" and they got you a towel and a bucket of water with which to take a bath, when what you really needed was the toilet! The people here will always remember you for your willingness to sit with them and learn to make sago baskets and local bags for carrying books and Bibles. They will also remember you for eating their foods with them, including *cassowary,* even if it did taste like the soles of your shoes. I don't think anyone ever found out that you were pushing some between the cracks in the floor for the dogs to eat.

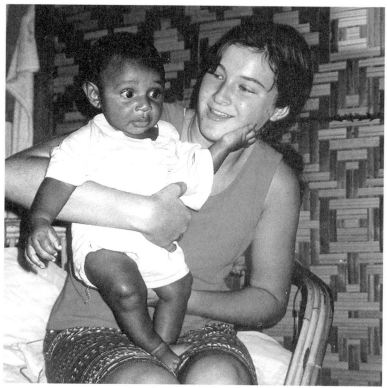

Rachel with Gouma, a boy her family almost adopted

Rachel making local food "sak sak"

They will also long remember your methods of dealing with their children. They will remember how you would quietly pick up a child and take them out of church to avoid disturbances when they cried. And when they threw fits because they did not get their way, you kindly and firmly held your ground, an example that has carried over to some of the parents to this day. They even say, "Tagiyato really showed us how to treat our children when we went to Daru for the Mini Congress." Your example of working with the kids was spread throughout the entire Western Province as more than 600 women watched you deal with their children.

And, yes you are still a legend at making sago. Remember the time you went to the bush with your friend Aina and made as much sago as the older women? Were they ever surprised! All the way home, Aina told everyone she saw how good you were at making sago. Remember how all the women would come and feel your arms and legs and comment on how strong they were? "You are a real Gogodala woman now!" they said. And then there was the time when you and Aunt Judy made sago when Aunt Judy visited us from America. The Gogodala women struggled to keep up with you. The next day they just rested in their houses because you wore them out with your rapid pace.

I can't forget the time when Mom had to go to Australia for her back problem and you took over all the household duties, taking very good care of your old dad. I will never forget the apple pies and brownies you made while she was gone. It was here in Papua New Guinea that you learned to make bread over a kerosene stove and learned to sew clothes from scratch on a treadle sewing machine.

Yes, you made a difference in PNG. No, you were not always cheerful, and yes, you were still a teenager, but your sacrifice to live here will have eternal results. Yet in everything about Papua New Guinea, the thing that is most precious to me is your note which still serves as a bookmark in my Bible. You had been asking me about salvation and you wanted to know how you could be assured of having it. Your note simply said, "Dad, I know now. I BELIEVE. Thank you so very much, Forever loving, Rachel."

Yes, Rachel, your time in Papua New Guinea was not wasted. You made a difference. And the difference was reflected even in your own life. Tagiyato, always keep God first! Continue to serve others. And never neglect your time with your Saviour. Thanks for being willing to spend your early teen years in Papua New Guinea. Yes, you made a difference!

Love,
Wawa (Dad)

1. Why do you think Rachel was such a good missionary in Papua New Guinea?
2. What was Rachel's father's favorite memory of Rachel during her time overseas?
3. Why do you think the natives liked Rachel so much?
4. How was Rachel a good example to the native women?

You are living with your parents as an overseas missionary. One day, you are walking through the village and spot a group of women watching their babies play in the dirt. This is not an unusual sight—children are often left alone to play on the ground—and you are about to walk by without commenting. Suddenly, however, you see that the babies are playing in animal manure, not just regular dirt! You're horrified! *How can you tell the mothers that they are endangering their babies' health without offending them or their local customs?*

1. Write a letter of appreciation to someone who works in a mission field (your pastor, an overseas missionary, or even a parent or teacher). List the things you appreciate about this person and tell them you see him or her making a real difference for God.
2. Read 1 Timothy 4:12. List the ways in which Timothy was supposed to be an example. Beside each way, write one concrete way you can be an example today.

32

A strong village native

The Reluctant Bride By John and Belinda Kent

"My daughter," Mombi said to Anna one summer day, "it is time for you to marry. I will begin negotiations with your husband's family next week."

The news fell like a lightning bolt on 14-year-old Anna's ears. She stared at her father in disbelief. "Father, are you sure?"

She had known this day was coming. In keeping with Iwam tradition, her husband had been picked out for her soon after her birth. But so *soon?*

Outside, the sky and trees looked as bright as ever, but their beauty was lost to Anna. "Are you sure?" she repeated again, unwilling to believe the news.

"Of course!" Mombi snapped. "I have said it, and it will happen. You know this is true."

Anna's face fell. How she longed for one of her 12 brothers and sisters to help her right now. She couldn't marry this man! Not only was he a non-Christian from another village, but *he was already married to another woman!* She thought about her new Christian religion and realized she had to stand for her beliefs.

"Father," she spoke into his brooding silence, "I cannot marry him."

Before she could explain, Mombi's face contorted in vicious anger. "What?" he screamed. "What makes you think you're better than the rest of your brothers and sisters?"

He leaped to his feet and strode toward her as she crouched by the cooking fire. His shadow blocked the light from the doorway as he raised his fist in the air and shook it threateningly. "Now, will you marry this man or not?"

"No, I will not," Anna sobbed through her tears.

Mombi was furious. For the next several months, despite Anna's protests, he continued negotiations with her future husband for an acceptable bride-price.

"His family will come for you this Sunday," Mombi informed Anna one weekday morning. "You'd better be ready."

Anna merely nodded. She had already planned her escape. Early Sunday morning she would flee to the jungle and escape the marriage.

I cannot betray my God, she thought to herself as she prepared for bed that night. *I cannot marry that man!*

Unfortunately, Mombi had other plans for his daughter's life. On Saturday seven men from her future husband's village arrived to watch her through the night. They slept in a circle around Anna, cutting off all hope of an early morning escape.

"Father," Anna pleaded early Sunday morning, "please don't send me away! This goes against my faith and my God!"

"No!" Mombi vehemently refused. "You have no choice in the matter. Men, take her away!"

The seven men leaped into action, grabbing Anna by her arms and legs and dragging her from the hut.

"No! No! You can't make me go!" Anna screamed, fighting her muscular captors. Her body twisted and writhed, but she was no match for them.

The men forced her into their canoe, thinking she would calm down on the water, but Anna only fought harder. In a last heroic effort she thrashed free of the men and capsized the canoe. In the flurry of water, bodies, and poles, Anna escaped

Anna

the men and fled into the jungle, dripping wet and afraid.

"What should we do?" the men asked Mombi when they dragged themselves from the river. He stood on the shore with his arms crossed.

"She's gone now," he told them bluntly. "You lost her. You'll have to come back next week and take her by surprise."

The men agreed and disappeared down the river in their canoe. "We'll get her next week," they promised each other.

But this was not to be. That same evening Mombi fell ill. During the following week Anna returned to the village. "God will help me. I am not worried," she said with confidence. Her faith in God provided a tremendous inspiration to the missionaries and other Christians in her village.

Then, the day before the seven men were scheduled to return, Mombi died of his illness. The wailing began that night and continued for several days as the villagers mourned his death.

Anna, too, mourned the loss of her father. But it was a bittersweet mourning. For now, at least, plans for her immediate marriage had been suspended. Although the final chapters of her story had not yet been written, Anna's faith remained strong, even in her sorrow.

1. Why didn't Anna want to marry the husband her father picked for her?
2. Why do you think Mombi was so insistent that Anna marry the man?
3. If you were one of Anna's Christian friends, what would you have told her to do?
4. How could Anna balance the advice in Exodus 20:12 and 2 Corinthians 6:14?
5. How do you think Jesus felt about Mombi's death?

Scenario

You are a missionary kid, living in a tiny village in Papua New Guinea. One day your friend Joe tells you that his parents want him to work in their business on the Sabbath. "If I don't help them," he tells you, "they will think I'm a bad son. They will probably punish me until I obey." He stares at the winding river, deep in thought, for a few minutes. Finally he speaks. "I think I should run away from home to escape their punishment. Will you help me get away?"

How will you respond?

Take Action!

Do you honor your parents? Is it ever all right to disobey your parents? If you have any issues you need to resolve with your parents, resolve them today!

Think of some friends you know who don't respect their parents. How can you show them the value of being respectful to one's parents? Put your plan into action.

Draw a small circle in the center of a piece of paper. Write the thing you are most loyal to inside the circle. Next, draw a larger circle around the small one. Inside the larger circle, write the thing you are most loyal to after the first thing. Repeat this process until you have listed all your loyalties. Decide if this is the way you want to live your life and if not, make the necessary changes on the paper and in your daily life.

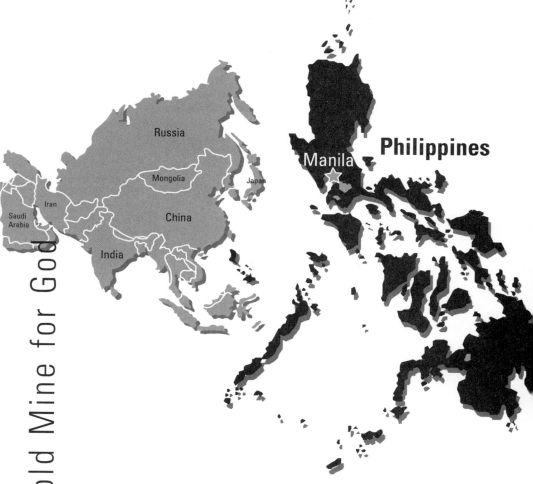

Russia

Mongolia

Japan

Iran

Saudi
Arabia

China

India

Manila

Philippines

Specs: The Philippines is a beautiful set of islands in the southeast Pacific Ocean. Its many volcanoes, beautiful beaches and jungles have led to its nickname, "The Pearl of the Pacific." Out of the approximately 168 different languages spoken in the Philippines, only 13 have the entire Bible translated, and 45 have portions of it. Because the Philippines is made up of so many islands and unique peoples, Adventist Frontier Missions has sent missionaries to several places.

Ifugao: The Ifuagao people live in the mountainous area of northern Luzon. These wet-rice agriculturists are famous for their ingenious system of irrigated terraces. Ifugao raise pigs and chickens but use them primarily for sacrificial purposes. The Ifugao live in small groups of 5 to 10 houses scattered among the rice terraces. Ifugao religion has an elaborate cosmology and more than a thousand deities of various classes. Ancestral and other deities are invoked in the case of illness or other difficulties with the aid of rice wine and feasting.

Mindoro: On the island of Mindoro, meaning "gold mine," the Mangyan tribal group, a quiet, reserved people, is considered extremely low-class. Their Filipino brothers often take advantage of them. To keep the peace, the Mangyans have retreated to the mountains, forsaking their fertile land to find an existence elsewhere. The Alangan tribe is a sub-culture of the Mangyan people and faces the same plight. Family groups are extremely important to the Mangyan people. Most *barangays* (small villages) are composed of family groups who live together in long houses on stilts. This protects them against flooding and some wild animals. Mangyans will eat almost anything—rice, beans, jungle leaves and tubers, monkeys, lizards, pigs, bugs, and larvae all sound tasty when you're hungry enough!

Palawan: Palawan, home of the Muslim Palawano, Molbog, and Jama Mapun people, is a long, isolated island in the southwest Philippines. Scattered settlements and shifting agriculture predominate, with rice as the main food crop. Corn, coconuts, beans, and sweet potatoes are also grown by the Palawano people.

DID YOU KNOW?

- The Philippines is the only Roman Catholic nation in Asia.

- Mangyans are so despised that bus drivers will often pull away quickly rather than let them ride their bus.

- Mangyans typically wear rice-sack or other cloth skirts (women) or G-strings (men). However, no clothing at all is also an option!

- A people called the Gaddang, closely related to the Ifugao, live in tree houses.

- The Philippines has more shoreline than the entire United States!

A typical hut in Ifugao

Ifugao, Philippines

The Ifugao people live in the mountainous area of northern Luzon, in the Philippines.

The Ifugao live in small groups of five to 10 houses scattered among the rice terraces. They are famous for their ingenious system of irrigated terraces.

Ifugao religion has an elaborate cosmology and more than a thousand deities of various classes. Ancestral and other deities are invoked, with the aid of rice wine and feasting, in the case of illness or other difficulties.

Ifugao raise pigs and chickens but use them primarily for sacrificial purposes.

Aaron Hatfield on another jungle adventure

33

S *nap!* Aaron Hatfield's eyes flew open at the sound of movement in the jungle. Visions of hungry jungle beasts filled his mind. He pulled his T-shirt closer around his body as though it could protect him from the unknown danger. But before long he'd forgotten his fears as a new enemy occupied his mind: cold.

After hiking a day in the jungle, Aaron had been damp with sweat when the sun had gone down. The dropping temperature had quickly chilled him until he felt colder than a scoop of hard vanilla ice cream. That reminded him of pumpkin pie and the Thanksgiving feast his family would enjoy without him this year. A sigh escaped his tightened lips.

"You awake?" Chester, the jungle guide, whispered between chattering teeth.

"Sure am," Aaron replied. "But I think Peter's sleeping like a baby."

Chester chuckled at the comparison.

"No, I'm not!" Peter's hoarse voice interrupted their mirth. "I'm just too cold to talk and too tired to hike."

Aaron had to agree. It had been a hard day for everyone. As the three men quieted down again, Aaron's mind replayed the adventure that had brought them to this clearing.

The hike had started at 11:00 that morning. "We'll be home by lunch," Chester had promised as he led them into the jungle. They had volunteered to visit a nearby spring that could be used as a water source for Buwao.

They had expected a short hike to their destination, but three hours later they finally stumbled onto the spring.

"What did I tell you?" Chester grinned, his white teeth shining like pearls in the dimly lit jungle. "A beautiful spring. And so close to the village!"

Aaron sighed. Chester had never owned a watch and probably didn't realize how far this water source really was. Surrounded by intense green foliage, the crystal-clear liquid was surprisingly cool and free of debris. And when Chester offered to show them a shortcut home, Aaron began to think that the spring held real hope after all.

"Follow me," Chester said as he bounded up a steep incline. "We'll climb up this mountain and then follow the ridge to the road."

Aaron couldn't object. It sounded simple enough. How could he have known that they would have to battle giant jungle vines with their machetes for most of the upward climb?

This is ridiculous, Aaron grumbled to himself as he swung his machete at a clump of leaves in his path. *This isn't exactly how I pictured spending the day before Thanksgiving.* But before he could give in to self-pity, a swarm of mosquitoes attacked him like a fleet of bomber planes. He spent the next several hours fighting them off.

When they finally reached the summit, Aaron began counting his steps so he'd know how far to walk up the mountain when he returned. *If I return,* he thought grimly. *I'm not sure one spring is worth all this effort.*

"Follow me." Chester's voice interrupted Aaron's reverie. "We're almost there."

"One . . . two . . . three . . . four . . ." Aaron tried to block out his homesick thoughts by concentrating on his steps. But after

1,962 paces Chester interrupted him again.

"I think we're lost."

Aaron looked up. He'd been watching his feet so carefully that he hadn't noticed that they'd reached the base of the mountain and had wandered in a valley for what must have been hours. The sun sat just above the horizon, and the three men's shadows had lengthened into 20-foot replicas of themselves.

Peter's shadow, which stretched across the clearing, scratched its head in confusion. "I agree with Chester. We'd better find a place to sleep for the night before it gets dark."

A huge sigh escaped Aaron's lips. "So much for counting my steps. Let's get moving."

Now, after two campsites and three failed attempts to build a fire, Aaron, Peter, and Chester huddled in a dry clearing and pretended to sleep.

Yes, Aaron concluded as he listened to the sounds of the jungle around him, *it's definitely been a day to remember.* His stomach growled insistently, and he clamped a hand over his stomach to quiet the noise.

A slice of pie sure would taste good, he mused to himself. *Or a plate of mashed potatoes and dressing.* He grimaced as his stomach rumbled again. *I'd even be happy with one tiny spoonful of cranberry sauce!* Visions of last year's Thanksgiving dinner flooded his memory, and his mouth began to water.

Here I am, lost in the jungle, when I could be sleeping in my comfortable bed in America. Why am I here? Who really cares about some hidden spring? I want fresh water and a Thanksgiving feast!

As the stars slowly moved across the dark sky, Aaron's complaints continued. Beside him Peter and Chester had fallen asleep. But rest would not come to Aaron's aching body and tortured mind.

God, help me! he finally pleaded. *Help me see a blessing in all of this frustration!*

The hum of a few persistent mosquitoes was all he heard. He slapped first his cheek, then his neck, then the back of his head. Finally the buzz of tiny wings disappeared into the night.

Thank You for sending the mosquitoes away, Aaron instinctively prayed.

And then it hit him. Thankfulness was what the Thanksgiving holiday was all about. How could he have forgotten? A smile crept to his lips. *Let's see . . . what am I thankful for?*

He stared at the cloudless sky. *Thank You, Lord, that it's not raining.* The ground beneath him caught his attention. In the jungle a dry patch of soil is as rare as a fruit tree in the desert. *And thank You for a dry place to sleep.* Aaron lay silent for a while, content for the first time since breakfast. Slowly the horizon came into focus. The sky above it grew lighter. The silhouettes of trees and vines appeared above him. Stars faded into grayness. And, to his surprise, the sun finally rose. *Thank You, God.*

Four hours later three tired, hungry men emerged from the jungle and stumbled onto a rutted road. Before long a truck rumbled by and they flagged a ride.

As the wind whipped through his hair, Aaron assessed his situation. He'd been in the jungle for 23 hours without food or shelter. He had nine leech bites, and countless tiny cuts and scrapes on his hands, evidence of the thorny vines he'd walked through. A burning sensation in his right arm reminded him of the nettles he'd brushed against the day before.

I may have bites, sores, and cuts, he thought with a grin, *but I've learned how to plead with God as I've never done before. I've learned the true meaning of Thanksgiving. And I've experienced an adventure that I'll remember forever.*

Aaron's stomach growled again, but this time he didn't complain. He knew he'd be back in the village soon, and he was sure a hot plate of rice and beans awaited him. *It's not exactly cranberry sauce and stuffing,* Aaron admitted to himself, *but it's close enough for me!*

Get Into the Action!

1. What things did Aaron miss about Thanksgiving Day?
2. Read 2 Corinthians 2:14. What could you have told Aaron to be thankful for?
3. What did Aaron learn to do that allowed him to smile in spite of his frustrating day?

One day, as you're passing the kitchen, you overhear a conversation between your mom and one of her friends.

"I'd like to take the family on a feed-the-homeless trip," your mom is telling her friend. "I think they've lost the true spirit of Thanksgiving. We could use all the money we would have spent on the dinner to buy supplies for the homeless, then spend the whole day working in the inner city. What do you think?"

You don't stick around to hear the friend's response, but you know that if your mom were to ask you how *you* felt, you wouldn't want to go. Miss fresh apple pie and creamy mashed potatoes? No way!

Several days later your mom approaches you with her idea. "What do you think?" she asks hopefully. *What will you say?*

List several of your favorite Thanksgiving traditions. Now imagine that you are spending Thanksgiving in the Philippines. How will your traditions change? How can you make the holiday special anyway? How will you show your true Thanksgiving spirit?

Pick a country on the globe, and look it up in the encyclopedia. Find out about one of the country's biggest holidays. How would you make a visitor from that country feel welcome at your house during the country's special holiday?

Read Luke 6:38, Acts 20:35, and 2 Corinthians 9:7. Why is it important to give, and what are the benefits of giving to others?

Read Ezekiel 36:26. What is the greatest gift God has given us? Now read Matthew 10:8. How should we respond to this gift? How will you respond to this gift?

Children love to swing in hammocks in Mindoro.

Mindoro, Philippines

On the island of Mindoro, which means "gold mine," the Mangyan tribal group, a quiet, reserved people, is considered extremely low-class. To keep the peace, the Mangyans have retreated to the mountains, forsaking their fertile land to find an existence elsewhere. The Alangan tribe is a subculture of the Mangyan people and faces the same plight.

Family groups are extremely important to the Mangyan people. Most *barangays* (small villages) are composed of family groups who live together in longhouses on stilts. This protects them against flooding and some wild animals.

Mangyans will eat almost anything. Rice, beans, jungle leaves and tubers, monkeys, lizards, pigs, bugs, and larvae all sound tasty when you're hungry enough!

Tim Holbrook displays his ever-ready medical bag.

The sharp three-inch thorn easily pierced the tough skin on top of Kapalatay's foot. It slid down at an angle, exiting near the ball of his foot under his big toe. Kapalatay collapsed in agony, pain shooting up his leg.

Seconds before, he had been chasing a stray chicken, yelling, "Come back here! Get out! Trap him against the house!"

The chicken had wheeled and darted, trying to avoid capture. Kapalatay had been running right behind it, twisting and turning, coming ever closer. Then he had tripped and fallen, and his foot had slammed down on a long bamboo thorn sliver, driving it completely through his foot.

Now Kapalatay lay on the ground, wondering what to do next. He had to get up and return to his hut or he'd never get help! Painfully he stood up on one foot and limped back home.

Once inside his hut he lay down and raised his throbbing foot. What should he do now? How would he finish his plowing? How would he harvest the *kamote* (sweet potato)? Kapalatay groaned again, realizing he wasn't going to be able to do much of anything for a while.

Several hours later and miles away from Kapalatay's hut, Tim and Dawn Holbrook trudged through brown knee-deep mud beneath a searing sun. With every step the oozing mess threatened to yank their sandals off their feet and send them plunging backward into the soft muck below. Occasionally they reached a small island of higher grass in a sea of mud, sand, and water.

"This business of crossing rice paddies doesn't suit me too well!" Dawn joked as she lifted a mud-laden foot, only to set it down again in the clinging slop. "I wish there was a quicker way to reach Pakpak village!"

"Me too," Tim agreed. "But it's just not safe to cross the Amnay River when it's flooded like this." He and Dawn had opted to take the long way to Pakpak, following a little-used trail and crossing a stronger, safer bridge.

"I know," Dawn said. "Better safe than sorry. But I'm worried about that man in Pakpak that Rodney told us about. The thorn in his foot sounds huge!"

Several hours earlier Tim and Dawn's student missionary had radioed in with news of Kapalatay's injured foot. The Holbrooks had filled their backpacks with antiseptics, scalpels, antibiotics, forceps, tweezers, and anything they thought might be useful in removing a large thorn. They had begun the trek to Kapalatay's house within a half hour.

Tim, who had just encountered a thornbush himself, rubbed his aching hand. "If I could live without any knowledge of thorns, I'd be perfectly happy," he announced wryly. "I feel sorry for the guy, Kapalatay."

An hour later, when he and Dawn finally reached Kapalatay's hut, Tim's sympathy for him grew even larger. The poor man lay moaning on the floor while Dawn gently sponged away the dried dirt and blood. Then she gently numbed the area around the entrance and exit wounds with lidocaine and cut into the swollen pocket of pus.

Tim watched in admiration as Dawn used forceps to probe the entrance hole, searching for the thorn. Blood oozed and seeped around the wound. Holding the flashlight steady with one hand, Tim used the other to grab some gauze and dab at the injured foot. Dawn continued probing the entrance and exit wounds, but no thorn could be found.

"Kapalatay," she said hesitantly, "I don't think there's any thorn inside your foot. It must have come out already."

Kapalatay shook his head vigorously. "You're wrong! I can feel the thorn inside. You've brushed against it several times!"

First Dawn, then Tim, took turns pushing the forceps into Kapalatay's foot, but neither missionary could locate the thorn. Deeper and deeper they probed, through layers of tendons, nerves, and muscles.

"Kapalatay," Dawn insisted again, "we really can't find the thorn!"

"But the thorn is in there!" Kapalatay argued weakly. "I can still feel it!"

Dawn was near tears. "I'm sorry," she told him quietly. "I just can't get it out. After a while, maybe it will come out to where we can see it."

This time Kapalatay merely moaned in agreement. His usually brown face looked pale from the pain. Dawn treated and wrapped his wound with a gauze bandage before speaking again. "Kapalatay, we're going to pray to our Father up in heaven now. We are going to ask Him to help you get better and make the thorn come out."

Kapalatay quietly bowed his head as Dawn offered a simple prayer. He watched in silence as the two missionaries departed.

Three or four days later someone from Pakpak appeared at the Holbrooks' door. "Pastor," he said excitedly, "do you know what happened to Kapalatay?"

"No, I don't," Tim responded. "What happened?"

"Well, the very next day after Ma'am prayed to our Father for help, Kapalatay looked at his foot and there was the thorn, sticking out of the top! He pulled it out with the tweezers he uses to pull his beard hairs out. Kapalatay says the thorn came out because Ma'am prayed to our Father up above. Kapalatay believes in Him, and he is so happy!"

The Holbrooks learned that the thorn had come out between Kapalatay's toes, nowhere near the holes on the top and bottom of his foot. Dawn had not seen a thorn sticking up between or near Kapalatay's toes, even though she had bathed the entire foot and examined it carefully. No thorn had been there. It had appeared only *after* she had prayed.

Kapalatay was indeed happy. His three-inch thorn had brought him a faith in the God of heaven that would continue to grow in the coming months. Tim and Dawn marveled once again at God's leading in their experiences in the mission field.

Get Into the Action!

1. How long was the thorn in Kapalatay's foot?
2. Why do you think things happened the way they did?

Scenario

You and your friend Amy are Christmas shopping in the mall. Amy finds the perfect gift for her brother, but when she gets to the cash register to buy it, she can't find her money anywhere! Somehow it has disappeared in the past several hours.

You pray together in the store, then go home to look some more. Several days later the money still hasn't turned up. Amy is a new Christian. *How will you explain the situation to her?*

Take Action!

Remember a time you tried to help someone with a medical problem. How did it go? How would you do things differently? If you still aren't sure what to do in a similar situation, ask a doctor for advice.

Pray for all the new Christians around the world.

Write out a list of things you could say or do that would help strengthen a new Christian's faith. Put them into action.

The Jeep That Ran on Water

By Tim Holbrook

The AFM jeep that ran on water. Villagers cram on until there's barely room to breathe.

The sun rose over the tops of the jungle trees on Sabbath morning, more blistering hot than the day before. But the church members in Buwao barely noticed. They were bubbling over with excitement. This was the day of the big baptism in the city of Sablayan, and they were going to go!

"Will there be lots and lots of people?" small children asked their mothers.

"Yes," the mothers responded, "and a visiting white-faced preacher who came all the way from America to talk to us!"

The children's eyes widened in disbelief.

"It's true!" older children took up the story. "He will tell us lots of stories, and then we will eat more food than we have ever eaten before. And after that, we will watch the baptism!" The older children forgot their maturity for a while and danced up and down in their excitement. "It's going to be a wonderful Sabbath!" they promised the younger children. "Just wait and see!"

Amid the commotion, dogs sniffed hungrily as the people built hasty cooking fires and cooked their meager breakfast. A line developed down by the pump as people took turns washing up. After collecting their food and packing it away, everyone set out for Baclaran, where the mission jeep was waiting.

They made their way single file down the winding trail, across rice-paddy dikes, and through plowed fields. Balancing carefully, they crossed log bridges that spanned soft gurgling streams.

Finally Baclaran came into sight. A cheer rose from the younger children as they raced toward the jeep parked by the side of the road. Almost before they knew it, every villager had loaded his or her belongings, Curtis Hartman had started the jeep, and they were bouncing off down the road to Sablayan.

Curtis whistled as he drove. He had also caught the excitement of this big adventure. He felt proud to be driving the mission jeep, and prouder still of the Buwao village church. He wanted to make sure that the members reached Sablayan in plenty of time to hear the sermon.

Curtis's brow furrowed in thought as he drove the jeep along the narrow road. There were two ways to get to Sablayan from Baclaran. One way would take them high up into the mountains, around many villages, through several precarious landslide areas, and then across the Patrick River on a cement bridge. The other way, a shortcut straight through the river valley, would cross the river repeatedly. Although this route could be dangerous, since the rainy season had started up again, Curtis knew it would cut an hour off their journey.

After a moment's thought Curtis chose the short river route. He saw that other vehicles had been crossing with no major problems, although there were a couple of deep crossings with soft sand that could give trouble to the unwary.

"Hang on!" Curtis called as the jeep started across the first river. Unbeknown to him, some river water got sucked up into the engine air intake, and somehow the oil filter cap popped off. Oil sprayed out all over the engine and front end. At each successive river crossing, more water poured into the air intake and into the open oil filter hole. Curtis drove on, oblivious to any of these happenings.

Ten miles (15 kilometers) later the faithful jeep pulled into Sablayan, still running smoothly. As Curtis parked the jeep, people swarmed down off the roof and poured out from inside. Cries of "We're here! We're here!" filled the air. The villagers quickly collected their things and set off for the ferry that would take them across to the Sablayan Adventist Church.

The church service was wonderful! Lots and lots of people crowded into the church or sat in clusters around the outside, trying to stay in the shade as they peered in through the open windows. Two TVs had been hooked up with a video camera so that everyone could see what was happening inside. A white-faced preacher who had come all the way from America told lots of stories. There was plenty of food to eat, and most important, there was a baptismal service. Four villagers from Buwao, along with more than 100 other people, were baptized in the blue-green waters of the South China Sea.

All too soon the sun made its way down toward the horizon. The Buwao church members gathered up their things, crossed the river to the waiting jeep, and began the trip home. Soon they reached the river valley. As they recrossed the river fords, the jeep continued to run as strong as ever. After dropping the people off at Baclaran, Curtis returned the jeep to Pandurukan and made his way home on his motorcycle. The jeep had traveled more than 28 miles (45 kilometers) since the first river crossing.

On Sunday morning Tim Holbrook needed to use the AFM jeep. But when he started the engine, he saw that there wasn't any oil pressure!

"Oh no!" Tim groaned. Since the jeep ran on oil-lubricated bearings, he knew he wouldn't be going anywhere soon. He shut off the truck and scrounged through the shed for the oil drain pan.

Within minutes he'd stationed himself flat on his back beneath the jeep. He carefully removed the engine drain plug. Glancing out from under the jeep, Tim spotted a forest of little wiggling brown legs. A crowd of eight dirt-smeared, smiling children grinned at him from above. Whenever Pastor did anything with the jeep, first-class entertainment was sure to follow! The children squatted down and fastened their gaze on the drain pan.

"*Pare!*" they all cried, commenting on the milk-white water that poured from the engine and filled the pan to the brim. Tim slid out from under the jeep and emptied the pan. The children chattered excitedly about the white-colored oil. They knew what used motor oil usually looked like.

"*Pare!*" they shrieked again as Tim filled a second pan with the runny white water. Again he emptied the pan and slid back under the mission jeep.

"*Pare! Dapo langis* ["There isn't any oil"]," they shouted as Tim filled a third pan with milk-colored water. He shook his head in astonishment. *Where's the oil?* he wondered, holding the pan under the drain and waiting for the oil to begin dripping out. Knowing that oil floats on water, he expected to see at least *some* oil in the engine.

Eighteen wide-opened eyes (including Tim's) watched as little black droplets of oil slowly welled up on the lip of the engine drain hole and went *plop, plop, plop* into the empty drain pan. Only one teaspoon of oil came out of that engine! One teaspoon along with three *gallons* of water!

Tim couldn't understand it. Normally the engine ran on two and a half gallons of oil. While the children watched, he replaced the air filter and oil filter and flushed the engine with oil three times before finally managing to get all the water out of the jeep's engine. Something was incredibly strange about the whole experience.

Before joining AFM Tim had worked as a mechanic for more than 20 years and had seen countless engines that had sucked up water. Usually rods were bent or broken, bearings were destroyed, and other major damage had occurred. He had never seen an engine run on a teaspoon of oil, let alone haul a jeepload of people for more than 28 miles (45 kilometers)!

Tim rejoiced as he thought about the miracle of the mission jeep that had run on water. He realized again that he served an awesome God. The same God who had hung the stars and placed the moon in the night sky, who had formed the craggy mountain peaks and made the tufted titmouse, the God who by His power kept untold trillions of electrons whirling ceaselessly around billions of atoms, was the same God who made the mission jeep run on water.

Get Into the Action!

1. Why were the people of Buwao so excited on the day of the trip? What event can you compare this to in your life?
2. Why do you think God let the mission jeep run on water?
3. How could Tim use this story to help the villagers see that God cares about their lives?

Scenario

Your friend April has just finished telling you a miracle story. She says an angel stopped her mother's car from hitting a semi while they were driving to school that morning. "I didn't see the angel," she concludes, "but I know he was there. I know God saved our lives."

What will you say to April? Do you believe in miracles?

Take Action!

Read Matthew 10:29-31. Rewrite the verse in your own words, substituting a different item for a sparrow.

Read John 14:11. Why are miracles such faith-building events? How would you define the word "miracle"? Look up the word in the dictionary and compare the definition with yours.

Write your own psalm, praising God for the miracles He has performed in your life. Skim through the Psalms to get a feel for how to write one.

Charcoal and Prayer By Tim Holbrook

Dawn helps treat a sick woman.

Sparks shot skyward and punched bright little holes into the inky mantle of darkness. Four fires spaced around a bamboo hut popped and crackled, their flames eating hungrily at the dry bamboo and branches.

In the flickering, wavering light, four men gripped blazing branches in their hands and ran back and forth between the fires and the hut, frantically flourishing the brands around and around. The branches looked like giant lanterns for a midnight celebration, but the looks on the men's faces were anything but joyful.

Inside the grass-roofed hut a flurry of activity shook the walls. Several people stuck their machetes down through cracks in the floor and walls and energetically rocked them back and forth. Smoke hung like a heavy gray blanket, curling around and smothering everything in the room. In the corner an old man waved burning gingerroot around the stomach of a woman who lay curled up on her sleeping mat.

Punsoray, the woman on the mat, groaned and

clutched her stomach. The people believed that evil spirits were causing her the pain, and they immediately redoubled their efforts at chasing them away. Punsoray had been fine at dinner, but now at 10:00 in the evening her pain had grown so intense that she could hardly keep from crying out.

Tanoy, the village *capitan* (chief), sat in a corner watching and thinking. This was the way to take care of the situation, wasn't it? Punsoray would be fine soon, they would see. But still, a small worry line creased his forehead. What was taking so long?

As the noise level rose, more and more people awoke and streamed into the big house, adding their own voices to the wild confusion of sound and activity. It hammered at the eardrums; it pulsed in the very marrow of the bones.

Marisa Miller, a student missionary, and her two Alangan friends also awoke and wandered into the already crowded house. They had been sleeping at the opposite end of the village, but the noise made rest impossible.

Marisa examined Punsoray. Something was definitely wrong. She stumbled down the trail to Tim and Dawn Holbrook's house as fast as she could.

"Dawn, Dawn!" she called at the door. "There is a lady over in Tanoy's house who has a problem with her stomach."

Dawn rolled over and sat up. "OK, I'll be there in a minute."

After dressing in the dark, Dawn grabbed her medical bag and, with the aid of her flashlight, made her way down the narrow path to Tanoy's house. There she found Punsoray curled up in a ball on her mat, moaning with pain.

Dawn looked at Tanoy, reading the hesitation in his sun-browned face. "Is it OK to treat her?" she asked, shouting to be heard above the din.

Tanoy nodded slowly, reluctantly. Dawn decided to try a dose of charcoal and mixed up a glassful in water. Helping Punsoray sit up, she held the glass for her as she swallowed. Punsoray made a weak, wry expression as the charcoal poured into her mouth and slid down her throat. Then she lay down again.

"May I pray?" Dawn asked loudly as she looked at Tanoy.

Tanoy nodded once more and heaved a huge sigh of defeat. Dawn prayed a simple prayer, asking God to heal Punsoray. Then she left the hut and stumbled back to bed.

Early the next morning Dawn walked down to Tanoy's house, wondering how Punsoray was feeling. Dawn entered the house quietly and looked around at all the mats for Punsoray's sleeping form, but she wasn't there. Fear gripped Dawn's heart. Where was she? Had she died, or had the family taken her somewhere? Surely they wouldn't try a spirit doctor so late at night! She began to ask everyone she met, "Where is Punsoray? Have you seen her today?"

Finally she found Milda, Tanoy's wife. "Where is Punsoray? Is she all right?"

Milda nodded her head happily. "Yes, she is fine now. She is working up on the mountain in her *kiengan* [mountain farm]."

Dawn caught her breath in wonder. Her patients usually didn't recover that quickly. Working up in the mountains was heavy work. When had Punsoray started feeling better? She shrugged her shoulders, walked back to the house, and forgot about the incident.

Several weeks later, while talking with a villager, Dawn discovered the answer.

"Do you remember when you prayed for Punsoray one night?" the villager asked her.

"Yes."

"Well, the next day the news was all over the village."

"What news?" Dawn's ears pricked up.

"Tanoy had been practicing his medicine on Punsoray for two hours without results. After your medicine and prayer, the pain left her completely within 15 minutes."

Dawn smiled all the way back to her house. It was clear to her—and the villagers—that she served an awesome God. Throughout the day she stopped her work often to praise Him for His miraculous healing power.

1. How do you think Tanoy felt when his "medicine" didn't work?
2. How do you think he felt when Dawn's medicine *did* work?
3. How might Dawn talk to Tanoy about this without hurting his feelings?

The phone rings just as you're crawling into bed.

"I'll get it!" you yell, and jump to the phone before your parents have a chance to respond. Your friend Mindy is on the other line, crying. Her parents have just told her they'll be getting a divorce, and she doesn't know what to do. Mindy doesn't know much about God, so you're sure she hasn't been praying about this tough situation. And you're *not* sure she'd even want to pray if you asked her.

What should you do?

What are some nonreligious coping mechanisms that people use in the following situations?

> Depression
> Anger
> Loneliness
> Family trouble
> Obesity
> A death in the family

Think of ways to incorporate God into the secular solutions you have listed. The next time someone talks to you about any of these problems, you will be prepared to help them.

Read 1 Thessalonians 5:17. How often do you pray? How often do you pray for other people? Next time you tell someone "I'll pray for you," *do it!* And do it right then! Ask the person if you can pray for them at that very moment. This will not only remind you later that you should continue to pray, but it will also mean a lot to the person you are praying for.

37

A Church Comes of Age By Dawn Holbrook

The church members wash one another's feet.

Dawn Holbrook's eyes flew open. Somewhere in the village a crowd of children had begun shouting at the top of their lungs. It was still dark outside. Was everything all right?

Tim groaned and rolled over. "There's our alarm clock," he mumbled into his pillow.

Suddenly Dawn remembered. It was only the village children, running around the basketball court. They were dragging empty plastic jugs and hollering at the top of their lungs for the joy of a new day.

She smiled and let their carefree shouts wash over her like music. She had grown to love these people. Her mind replayed a collection of familiar scenes from the village. Parents rocking little ones to sleep, their changing song loud enough to be heard at the other end of the valley, their swinging hammocks rocking their houses as well. Villagers calling from house to house, passing along the latest gossip and jokes. Babies crying inconsolably during church because their mothers' full attention was on the story. Toddlers running back and forth on the side porch or banging their tiny fists on the hollow-sounding door. And moms smiling indulgently at their "naughty" children and pulling them unceremoniously into their laps to nurse and quiet them.

A contented sigh escaped Dawn's lips. Yes, she loved these noisy, happy, sometimes rowdy people of Mindoro.

But, she wondered as the outside shouts continued, *do they understand reverence? Do they ever quietly reflect on their individual Christian experience? How will they react to a deeply reverent commitment service?*

She thought of the church's first Communion service, to be held this Sabbath. *What will they do? What will they think?* Countless questions crossed her mind, and she realized with a start that she would soon know the answers. Communion was the next day!

Sabbath dawned as bright and sunny as usual.

"Do you think they're ready?" Dawn whispered to Tim just before church.

He flashed her a mischievous grin. "They'd better be! We've drilled the routine into them."

Despite her worries Dawn had to laugh. It was true. Wednesday's prayer meeting, Friday's vespers, and that morning's Sabbath school had all been devoted to Communion service preparations. Dawn and Tim had demonstrated the foot-washing process, the passing of the bread and wine, and the times of prayer and reflection.

"The Holy Spirit will be present. This is a time to be reverent," Tim had told them again and again. The villagers had nodded and smiled, but did they really understand?

As usual, they had asked plenty of questions. "Can I share with my toddler?" one mother had asked.

"How does grape juice cleanse us inside?" a thoughtful man had wondered.

"Can I hold and nurse my infant during church?" a deaconess had asked as she made the unleavened bread with Dawn.

But all the questions gave Dawn no clue as to how the villagers would act during Communion. She scanned the church as the members assembled for worship. The day had begun as usual. Villagers had bathed and pounded their morning rice early in order to be ready for church.

Sabbath school had been normal too. A crowd of villagers had drifted onto Tim and Dawn's porch during song service. Babies cried. Toddlers ran back and forth on the porch, banging on the door. But the people had kept coming.

Twenty members of nearby lowland churches had come with the elder to share the service. Tim had returned with the jeep full of people from Buwao and Mayba. The crowd had spilled around the corner onto the small side porch and filled it as they listened to more stories about the Last Supper and Communion. Sabbath school was dismissed with the admonition for each member to search his or her heart, and if there was an unconfessed sin, to confess it to God and the injured party before church.

Dawn squeezed Tim's hand just before he stood to call church to order. Already she noticed a change in the group. There was no shuffling for seats, no toddlers running around unnoticed, no crying babies, no whispering adults and teens.

Are these the same people? she wondered for a moment.

When an elder dismissed the villagers for foot washing, they filed past another elder, a deacon, and Tim for their basin and towel *in complete silence!* Quietly they moved out into the yard in pairs and after individual prayers washed each other's feet.

Tears came to Dawn's eyes as she watched the reverence of each person. *This must be close to how it was in the upper room,* she mused to herself. *Clean bodies and hearts, but dirty feet from walking in the mud and dust.* Quietly they filed back onto the porch.

"We'll distribute the bread to you now," an elder informed the waiting group, "and then we'll pray." Every head bowed and every tongue remained silent. Together with the elder, the church members ate the bread and joined him in prayer. The same routine accompanied the wine ceremony.

How long can this last? Dawn wondered in awe.

Just before the closing song and prayer, Tim introduced a brief period of thanksgiving and testimony. Again and again

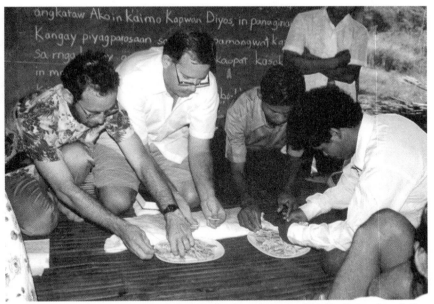

Curtis Hartman (student missionary, left), Tim Holbrook, and other church members break the bread for Communion.

the people gave thanks for their new understanding, this special service, and the gift of Jesus.

After the closing song Dawn breathed a sigh of relief. It was over! But no one wanted to leave. They quietly visited and wished each other a happy Sabbath again and again. They seemed to want to linger in the place and mood of the service. Finally as babies and children got restless, they drifted away to their homes.

On Sunday morning Dawn awoke to the sound of children running around the basketball court, dragging plastic jugs, and shouting at the top of their lungs. Houses rocked in rhythm to the chanting songs of adults holding babies. Men and women called from house to house. Dawn smiled contentedly. Although life in Pandurukan seemed to have returned to normal, she knew the Adventist church had taken a giant forward step in maturity.

1. Why do you think the villagers were so reverent during Communion?
2. Do you think the church members were that quiet the next week at church?
3. What do you think the church members learned from the experience?

Sabbath morning dawns in beautiful shades of pink and orange, but you hardly notice. You're worried about taking Pedro to church with you this morning. Just last night you found out that today was Communion Sabbath.

Great, you think. *On top of everything else, I'll have to explain Communion.* And you're right. When you get to church, Pedro is completely confused.

"Wine?" he asks incredulously. "I thought Christians didn't drink wine! What's going on here?"

You take a deep breath and prepare to explain the idea of Communion to Pedro in a way he can understand. *How will you tell him about it?*

Read 1 Corinthians 11:28. Even if you are not able to participate in Communion yet, you can still watch it with the right attitude. Next time your church celebrates Communion, prepare your heart by confessing all your sins and making any misunderstandings right between you and others. Try to notice if Communion impacts you more because of your preparation.

Spy on yourself! Next Sabbath in church, notice how reverent you are. Compare this with your record for the past several weeks. Are you showing respect to God by your attitude during church? Work on being continually more reverent in church.

Is there more than one way to be reverent? How do you feel the most reverent? Ask your family when they feel the most reverent, and record what you find. Practice any new ideas you may have learned.

38

Bistasio with his two children

Bistasio yawned and stretched his arms in the early-morning light. It seemed as if he had just fallen asleep! He rolled out of bed, grabbed his ax, and made his way down the ladder to chop firewood. A pale, translucent gray haze hung over the village as smoke from cooking fires floated softly in the air. After chopping an armful of kindling, he gathered it up and climbed back up into his hut.

While Bistasio built a cooking fire on the dirt- and rock-covered section of the bamboo floor, Marcolita, his wife, pounded the morning's rice in a wooden mortar carved from a log. She hammered off the rice husks, quickly tossed the rice in the air to remove the chaff, and dumped the rice into a black kettle.

Roosters crowed as they pecked and scratched among the cast-off rice husks. Dogs cautiously sniffed the morning air, and several carabao calves sounded their cries. Mushmeng, the silky black goat, playfully butted a hut post, shaking the whole house.

Bistasio settled down to watch the rice cook. He

would eat a good meal, because today he was hiking to the mountains for posts. He wanted to build a new house before the rains came. The hut felt a bit looser each time Mushmeng butted it. *The termites and ants have to eat too,* he thought with a wry grin.

After his breakfast of rice and a few cooked greens, Bistasio tied his *pisao* (machete) around his waist and, clad only in his loincloth, began hiking up the Makatikon River valley, searching for hardwood trees of just the right size. Higher and higher he climbed, scaling the rugged rocky walls inch by inch. The rippling stream gradually gave way to rough dry gravel.

Bistasio found himself entering a narrow canyon. Towering sheer rock walls rose abruptly on both sides, and the streambed narrowed almost to a point at the far end. It looked like a dead-end canyon. But as he made his way along the dry streambed, he spotted some trees far above him that looked to be exactly the right size.

Reaching the end of the canyon, Bistasio began climbing the dry waterfall. His bare feet and toes gripped the small jutting ledges as he reached above his head to find handholds. Slowly he made his way up almost 50 feet to a wide ledge. It looked like a shelf chiseled into the vertical rock wall. Massive walls loomed close on each side.

Bistasio decided to rest his aching muscles for a few minutes before continuing up the wall. He didn't know that beady black eyes were following his every movement. He didn't know that a dapang viper was slithering down the canyon, its long black tongue flicking in and out, searching among the loose rocks and gravel for frogs, mice, birds, or anything else that looked edible. Its inky black scales rippled along its eight-foot-long, five-inch-thick body. Its venom could kill a human in just four seconds.

Unaware of the snake's presence, Bistasio looked up along the rock wall and began to plan his route to the top. Suddenly he saw an enormous black snake speeding down the dry waterfall, hurtling directly toward him. He knew at a glance that it was deadly poisonous and would reach him in seconds. He had no time to draw his *pisao.*

Screaming, he covered his face with his hands and cried out, "Lord, Your will be done!"

Bistasio in his hut with Marcolita and one of their children

Bistasio opened his eyes, awaiting certain death. But the snake was gone!

Frantically he looked around the ledge. No snake. It couldn't have reversed its course and gone back up the near-vertical dry waterfall—there hadn't been enough time. He turned and scanned the streambed far below, but no long black body could be seen. Climbing down and searching among the rocks at the bottom revealed nothing either. The snake had just vanished!

Bistasio shared this story during thanksgiving time at church that week. He didn't know if the snake had somehow made it to the bottom and hidden under the rocks or if an angel had grabbed it away. But he did know that God had saved him from certain death on the mountainside.

"For he will command his angels concerning you to guard you in all your ways; they will lift you up in their hands. . . . You will tread upon the lion and the cobra" (Psalm 91:11-13).

1. If you were a missionary in Mindoro, what kind of house would you build?
2. What are some of the dangers you face on a daily basis that God may have protected you from in the past?
3. Describe a time when you know God saved you from danger or death.

You sit in the waiting room, anxiously picking at loose threads on your jeans. Your mom waits beside you, silent and distant. You're both afraid. You've been having strange stomach pains for over a year now, and the doctors have promised that they'll give you their diagnosis today.

Several minutes later the doctor emerges and motions you into his office. "I hate to tell you this," he begins quietly, "but things don't look good. The disease you have will kill you within three months."

Your mom gasps, but you can't even respond. You? About to die? It doesn't seem real! *How will you spend the last three months of your life?*

Look up Mindoro in the encyclopedia or on the Internet, and see if you can find any information about how the people who live there build their houses.

Try cooking brown rice, preferably over an open fire. Better yet, visit a specialty health foods shop and find unhusked rice so you can break the husks off for yourself.

39

Lunito

Lunito's eyes opened wide in fright. Every muscle in his body tensed. He was barely breathing as the huge insect hovered in front of him, waiting. Even in the darkness of his hut, Lunito could see the insect's size. Its body was as thick as his wrist, and its angry buzz filled his hut. This was obviously not an ordinary jungle insect. He had seen one of them in the past and knew what it meant.

As the giant insect slowly circled his sleeping mat, Lunito turned his head to follow. What should he do? Why was it coming for him?

Suddenly, in a lightning blur of a movement, the insect darted in, bit him hard on his left shoulder, and disappeared. Piercing pain shot through his arm and chest, and he collapsed onto his mat, clutching his shoulder and writhing in agony.

He already knew that no medicine could heal him. Lunito lay on his mat and searched his mind for someone who could have sent the curse. He knew that someone had cast a spell on him.

The Curse By Tim Holbrook

Slowly Lunito remembered. Four weeks ago he had talked to Zito about buying some pineapple plants. He'd always wanted a small pineapple field, and Zito had 100 plants to sell. They had worked out a price, and Lunito had agreed to pay her on Sunday and pick up his plants the following day.

But for some reason Lunito had been busy that Sunday. Later in the week he had caught up with Zito to talk with her again about the plants. She had been a little upset, but had agreed to meet him the next Sunday instead.

Once again Lunito was busy and missed his appointment!

"Do you want my plants or not?" Zito had asked him angrily the next time she saw him.

"Of course I do! I'll meet you next Sunday, I promise!" But even though Lunito wanted those plants more than anything, he forgot to meet Zito for the *third time* in a row. Zito was furious, and Lunito was ashamed.

"You'd better get your plants and pay me this Saturday, or you'll be sorry!" she stormed.

Lunito's heart fell. "But I worship my God on that day," he had tried to explain. "I can't buy them on the Sabbath. If you'd just let me wait until Sunday . . ."

But Zito wouldn't hear of it. She had walked away in a huff, leaving Lunito to ponder what she might do. Zito had a reputation for being an *abolario* (witch doctor), and Lunito knew all about the things that *abolarios* were capable of. After all, he had been one himself before he had become an Adventist.

Shooting pain coursed through Lunito's arm, bringing him back to the present. "Zito has cursed me!" he said to himself.

He had seen this kind of bug before, when he had been a witch doctor. He knew what it could do to the person it bit. But surely Jesus was more powerful than any curse.

Lunito tried to work, but as the days dragged by, he became weaker and weaker. The pain in his shoulder and back made walking difficult. His head hurt, and even taking a pain reliever didn't help. Every night and many times during the day Lunito prayed that Jesus would bring healing to him.

"My family needs food," he pleaded as he tossed and turned

on his sleeping mat at night. "But I just don't have the energy to work!"

Days passed. Lunito became weaker and more discouraged. The pain had spread from his shoulder to his entire body. He had to fight to simply sit or stand.

One night about a week after the bite, Lunito finished his prayers and lay down on his mat feeling depressed. "Jesus, why haven't You healed me? I know You are more powerful than the devil, but . . ."

Lunito's prayer drifted off as he fell into a troubled sleep and began to dream. In his dream Lunito saw Pastor Panghulan, the head Adventist pastor for Mindoro Occidental. Pastor Panghulan was dressed in shimmering white clothes, and an angel stood beside him. The light from the two of them was so bright that Lunito had to shade his eyes.

"Lunito," the angel in his dream spoke softly, "you cannot be healed until Pastor Panghulan prays for you."

Before Lunito could request a prayer, the pastor began to pray for him. A deep sense of peace filled him as the pastor's plea for healing rose to heaven.

Suddenly Lunito awoke. Something was different. The pain— it was gone! He stood up and flexed his shoulder and worked his neck muscles. There was no pain at all. He was healed!

Immediately Lunito dropped to his knees and thanked the Lord for His healing presence. "Jesus, I knew that You were more powerful than any curse," Lunito said with his head bowed. "But I allowed myself to doubt You. Please forgive me for not trusting You completely. Thank You for making me well again."

With a smile on his face Lunito lay back down on his mat, knowing that he'd sleep well that night. After this experience curses would never scare him again.

1. Why do you think it was easy for Lunito to doubt God's power in his life?
2. Against whom are we really struggling? (Ephesians 6:12.)
3. What kind of shield would have helped Lunito face the curse and his fear? (Ephesians 6:16.)
4. What could Lunito have done differently to keep Zito as a friend?

You're walking with a friend when suddenly a black cat runs right in front of you.

"Oh no," your friend moans, obviously afraid. "Something bad will happen to us very soon!"

What will you say?

Make a list of all the "faith texts" you can think of. Hang them on your wall to remind you that you have nothing to fear.

Pray for people in Mindoro, such as Lunito, who live with constant reminders of their spirit-worshiping past.

List customs or expressions you know of that refer to a power other than God. (Example: "Knock on wood," Friday the thirteenth). Think of a new phrase or action that will show your allegiance to God instead. Practice honoring Him by using your new ideas instead of the old ones.

Ramon

40

Ramon jumped up and down in excitement. His bright shiny eyes stayed riveted on the book in Lunito's hands. He could hardly believe it. He had seen books from a distance down in the barrio and had been amazed at the words that came from them. He had longed to live near someone who actually owned a book and could make it talk.

Ramon's remote village lay far back in the rugged mountains of central Mindoro. Its cluster of thatched bamboo huts were nestled in a snug little valley, kept green from a sparkling spring of water that meandered down the mountain.

Here lived wrinkled and toothless old grandmothers whose shoulders were humped from years of carrying baskets of *nami* (cassava) up steep mountain slopes. Their husbands, the *matanda* (old men), were revered for their wisdom and witchcraft skills. They looked distinguished, with silvery hair and sometimes a few wisps of white scraggly beards.

Skillful young men and women wove baskets,

Chosen, Part 1 By Tim Holbrook

hammocks, and bamboo mats to sell in the barrio. Many laughing, singing, and playing children invented ingenious games, squabbled over bamboo toys, and swung for hours at a time in woven hammocks suspended from the rafters. As they swung, they sang at the top of their lungs.

Pigs rooted and grunted in the dirt under the houses. Chickens scratched the dirt and snatched up insects, hardly stopping their routine to lay eggs in nooks and crannies. Dogs barked and growled, keeping their wary eyes out for possible intruders. All in all, it was a happy, healthy Alangan village.

Ramon was content in his village. He had just married a beautiful girl named Dulion. He had built himself a strong little hut and felt that he was making his way in life. Still, he had an undying longing to learn to read.

Now Lunito actually owned a book. A Bible! Perhaps he could learn to make it talk. "Where did you get it? Who gave it to you? Did you buy it?" Ramon could hardly contain himself.

"A missionary down in town gave it to me. He said that I could have it because I can read. Here, I'll show you."

Lunito proudly opened the Bible and, slowly tracing the words with his fingers, read out loud in Tagalog, *"Nang simulang likhain ng Diyos ang lupa at ang langit* ["In the beginning God created the heavens and the earth"]."

Fascinated, Ramon let his eyes follow Lunito's moving finger as it pointed out the words.

"Read some more," he implored when the finger came to a stop.

"OK. 'Then God said, "Let us make man in our image."'"

"Oh," breathed Ramon, "that's wonderful. I wish I could learn to read like that. Will you teach me, Lunito?"

Lunito shrugged. "If I have time. I'll tell you what. Every time I read, you watch the words as I point them out and try to make the same sounds I am making. Maybe then you can learn to read."

From that day on, every chance Ramon had, he watched as Lunito read the Bible and pointed out the words. As the days turned into months, and the months into years, the lessons became a tradition. After the sun sank behind the mountains and as the refreshing cool breeze swept up from the river, the two men sat together around a crackling fire and read the Bible.

Three years passed. Ramon continued to practice reading and also tried to write out the words from the Bible. He began to read slowly by himself, and he developed a scrawl that was hardly legible. "I want to read as fast as I can talk, and I want to write quickly and neatly," he told his wife again and again.

By this time Ramon had read through the entire Bible on his own. He didn't understand many things, but as he read the conviction grew in his heart that *Panginoon* (God) really had made the world, and that He was more powerful than the myriads of spirits who ruled the Alangan life.

The stories in the Bible told of people who prayed to God for help, and God had answered their prayers. Why not see if this God would help him? Ramon decided to find out.

"Panginoon," he prayed, *"I want to learn to read as fast as I can talk, and be able to write quickly and neatly. Please help me to accomplish this. Amen."*

The years slipped by. Ramon continued to read Lunito's Bible every day and often far into the night. He usually read out loud to clusters of sleepy children and to listening mothers and fathers who had gathered around the fire.

Slowly his speed increased. His writing skills also improved, and the older men started asking him to write messages and notes to people down in the barrio. The day came when Ramon could actually read faster than the people listening could understand. They begged him to slow down! God had answered his prayer.

One night, as Ramon and the villagers were gathered around the fire, he overheard a conversation between a visitor from the village of Pandurakan and an older man.

"A missionary and his family are living in Pandurakan now," the man said. "They give medicine to people who are sick. They also pray to *Panginoon* and worship every Sabbath. They teach lots of interesting things out of the Bible."

Ramon pricked up his ears at that. A missionary in Pandurakan? Worship? Praying to *Panginoon?* Ramon visited

Pandurakan as soon as he could to see if this was true. Sure enough, the visitor had been right. There *were* missionaries living there, and they *did* worship on Sabbath and pray to *Panginoon.*

After his first visit Ramon often went back to listen and observe. He felt a growing desire to live in Pandurakan and learn about *Panginoon.*

One special Sabbath some visitors brought a generator and a television to Pandurukan and showed a movie about Jesus. Ramon sat as if glued to the ground, absorbing every word and every picture in the movie. Again the feeling of longing washed over him. *Oh, how I wish I could live here and learn more about Jesus,* he thought wistfully.

Ramon sat up straight. Why not? If his wife was willing and the elders agreed, he would move to Pandurukan immediately.

However, the elders didn't want Ramon to leave. In the Alangan culture the elders' words are law, so Ramon stayed. But he continued to pray. Every night after he read Lunito's Bible, he prayed the same thing. "God, I want to live in Pandurakan. I want to learn more about You and to have someone who can explain the things from the Bible that I can't understand."

One night, as he lay on his bamboo mat on the rough floor, Ramon had a dream. Jesus stood before him. He knew it was Jesus because He looked exactly like the Jesus from the video the visitors had shown. Jesus was clothed in a white light so brilliant that it hurt Ramon's eyes to look at Him. Overcome by the sight, Ramon dropped to his knees, bowed his head, and began to weep.

Gently Jesus asked him, "Why have you called Me?"

"Oh, Jesus," Ramon sobbed out, "I want to live in Pandurakan so I can go to church and learn the answers to my questions. I want to study the Bible."

Jesus answered in words that were filled with compassion. "Don't worry, Ramon. You will move there soon." He pointed over His shoulder in the direction of Pandurakan.

The dream slowly faded, and Ramon awoke. He was at peace. Jesus had told him he would be able to move to Pandurakan.

Time went on. Ramon continued to read and study his Bible,

but many unanswered questions swirled around in his mind. What did this text mean? And that one? There was so much to learn.

Then disaster struck.

One day as his wife, Dulion, rocked back and forth in her hammock, she fell to the floor unconscious. When she awoke, she couldn't feel or move the left side of her body. Her feet twitched sporadically as if some cruel prankster was in control of them. Her breathing became hard and raspy as she struggled to pull air into her lungs.

Ramon was terrified. "What's wrong? What's wrong, Dulion?" he shouted. "Why can't you stand up? Why can't you breathe?"

"I don't know, Ramon. I've lost all feeling in my left side," Dulion panted, gasping painfully in her attempts to breathe.

Ramon instinctively dropped to his knees and began praying for Dulion's healing.

But as the days slipped into weeks, Dulion's paralysis remained. She still had difficulty breathing, and she couldn't even sit up in her hammock.

"Don't worry, Ramon," the village elders said. "We know what to do. We will collect seaweed and ginger and perform the rituals. You have many chickens we can use to pray to the spirits. All will be well. You'll see."

That night the elders gathered around Dulion's mat. A low-burning fire dimly lit the little hut. They waved several bowls of smoking ginger around her feet, legs, chest, and head, adding a dusky incense to the already pungent aroma of the room. They placed dried burning seaweed next to her mat, and someone sacrificed a chicken on her behalf. Mixed with the smoky haze, the chanting and muttering of the elders filled the room as they asked the spirits for healing. But despite all the rituals Dulion remained paralyzed.

"Don't worry, Ramon. We'll try again," the old men promised. They huddled together to discuss what they should do next.

Over the next several weeks the elders performed many different ceremonies. They killed many chickens and made countless entreaties to the spirits, but nothing solved Dulion's problem. The old men pondered some more.

"Ramon, you will have to stop reading the Bible," they told him. "Dulion is not getting well because you are reading the Bible."

Ramon was devastated. Stop reading the Bible? How could he? Yet he wanted his wife to recover. At last he reluctantly agreed to stop. But late at night after everyone was asleep, he pulled his blanket up over his head and, by the light of his flashlight, read from Lunito's Bible and prayed to Jesus for Dulion's healing. The days passed into months, and still Dulion's condition didn't change.

"Ramon, you *have* to stop reading the Bible," the elders insisted. "Don't you want your wife to get well? We are doing all this work for her, and you aren't even trying to help!"

Reluctantly Ramon agreed. He picked up the Bible and slowly walked to a cluster of large rocks. He dug under one of them and buried the Bible.

Three months passed. Ramon did not read the Bible or pray. The elders continued Dulion's treatments with no results. Before long, Ramon sank into discouragement. *Perhaps the old men are right and there's nothing to this Jesus,* he thought. *If Jesus cares about me, why hasn't He answered my prayers?*

(to be continued)

Get Into the Action!

1. Why was Ramon initially interested in reading Lunito's Bible?
2. Read Hebrews 4:12. Why do you think the Bible had such an impact on Ramon even though he had no one to explain it to him?
3. Ramon believed in *Panginoon*. Why, then, did he agree to stop reading his Bible?
4. Why didn't the elders want Ramon to move to Pandurukan?

One day, during lunch break at your public school, Mrs. Wheaten approaches you. "Listen," she says. "I've noticed that you pray before your meals." You smile, hoping she's a Christian like you. Mrs. Wheaten doesn't smile in return.

"In our school we want all students to feel equal," she tells you slowly. "When you pray in public like that, it makes some students nervous." She stops and stares out over the crowded lunchroom before continuing. "If you want to keep attending this school, you'll have to stop praying over your meals."

How will you respond?

Many villagers like Ramon and Lunito have never seen a "talking book" or held a Bible in their hands. What can you do to help them? Try raising some extra money and donating it to a Bible-translation or Bible-supplying program in a foreign country. Your pastor should know of some great projects you can help out with.

Read Matthew 4:4. Is reading the Bible as important to you as eating? To remind yourself to spend time in God's Word, keep a Bible in the kitchen. Ask your family if you can read a verse or a chapter to them before at least one meal a day. Or if you eat alone, read the Bible while you eat.

Record your favorite Bible passages onto tapes. Listen to them in the car or give them as gifts to friends or shut-ins.

41

Ramon, Dulion, and their child

Chosen, Part 2 By Tim Holbrook

W*hat's happening:* Ramon borrows Lunito's Bible and learns how to read. He learns about *Panginoon* (God) and discovers that there are missionaries in Pandurukan. More than anything, Ramon wants to move there, but the village elders tell him that he must stay where he is.

One night Ramon has a dream in which *Panginoon* tells him he will be able to move to Pandurukan. Then Ramon's wife, Dulion, gets very sick. In order to heal her, the elders make Ramon promise to stop reading his Bible and praying. Ramon obeys them and buries his Bible under a rock.

* * *

That night Ramon had another dream. He was standing in absolute darkness, and as he looked around in bewilderment, he saw a small hole. It was about a foot in diameter, and a glorious light shone through it. Although the light shone from a distance, it was such a wonderful light that instant longing filled Ramon.

He wanted to move toward it, but the darkness

stopped him like a thick black wall. No matter how hard he pushed and strained, he couldn't reach the light.

"Oh, please, God, I want to go to the light," Ramon prayed.

Soon the light began to travel toward him, increasing in intensity until he could hardly bear to watch it. He stood still, letting the light wash over him in a glistening shower of glorious radiance.

Closer and closer the light came, still shining through the small hole like a beacon. Ramon strained to reach it. And then it was on top of him, cascading over him, and warming his very soul. It filled the darkness until there was no more. For a moment Ramon stood covered in total transcendent whiteness. Then slowly the light continued passing by and receded into the distance. Once again Ramon faced the black night alone.

Ramon woke up with a start and stared around his hut. The light from his dream had been so bright that for a time he couldn't see around him. Slowly his sight returned, and with it the renewed desire to read the Bible.

Early the next morning Ramon retrieved the Bible from under the rock and began his daily reading and praying. The elders didn't say anything. It was as if they knew that their treatments had failed and that Ramon wouldn't harm anything by reading his Bible. Dulion's condition remained unchanged.

One evening, as Ramon read from the Old Testament, he noticed that all the patriarchs had built altars to God before praying. Adam, Noah, Abraham, Jacob, and the children of Israel had all built altars.

Why not me? he thought. A tingle of excitement coursed through his body. *It surely can't hurt.*

Early the next morning Ramon hiked far into the forest and began constructing his altar. Carefully he carried stones and placed them in position until he had built an altar about two feet high and two feet square. It was perfect.

Ramon knew what to do next. He dropped to his knees, clasped his hands together, and poured out his request for Dulion's healing. Tears streamed down his face as he pleaded with God. Time seemed to slow down and then stop for Ramon.

He didn't know how long he knelt there, but a peace slowly settled in his heart. God had heard his prayer, and He would answer.

Finally Ramon stood up and stretched his stiff muscles. After one last look at his altar he quietly made his way home. *When will God answer my prayer?* he wondered excitedly. *By the next rainy season, I hope.*

When Ramon walked into his hut, Dulion was sitting upright by the fire! The hair on the back of Ramon's neck stood up.

"Dulion, you're sitting up! You're well! When, uh, how, uh, did this happen?" he stammered.

"A little while ago," Dulion said calmly. "I just felt like sitting up. I can breathe fine now. See?" She sucked in a great lungful of air.

"I'll have supper cooking in a few minutes," she said, and busied herself with preparing the meal from a sitting position. Her dark eyes twinkled with delight at Ramon's surprised expression.

Ramon sat down and thought over his day. The miracle must have happened while he was praying. God *had* heard his prayers. Joy flooded over him. God cared about him after all!

The next day Dulion started to walk. She had to be very careful, because during the long months of paralysis her muscles had weakened and shriveled. However, as the days sped by and she continued to exercise, her strength gradually returned until she was walking and working as if she had never been ill.

As life settled back down again in the village, Ramon's desire to move to Pandurukan returned. He continued to pray about the problem, but the elders still refused to let him leave.

One evening after Ramon had closed his Bible for the evening, one of the villagers brought out his prized possession, a transistor radio, and turned it on. Looks of astonishment and wonder swept over everyone's face. The whole village eagerly clustered around to hear the music and talking that came from thin air. They soon discovered that the radio played continuing stories. As the days passed, the whole village looked forward to nightfall so they could hear the next captivating episode.

After the story one evening Ramon borrowed the radio. As he scanned the different stations, a program caught his attention.

He listened as a doctor from Manila gave instructions on how to make medicines from herbs and roots and tree bark. Fascinated, Ramon listened to the whole program. Many of the trees and roots that the doctor mentioned grew farther back in the mountains. *I wonder if it really works,* he thought idly to himself.

The next day many children in the village got sick. Ramon instantly recognized their symptoms from what the radio doctor had described.

"I'll be back as soon as I can," Ramon told the worried village elders. "I think I can fix the problem."

He raced into the forest to collect the bark and roots he needed to make the medicine the doctor had prescribed. When he returned, he gave the children the medicine and prayed for their healing.

By the next morning almost all the children had recovered. Although Ramon felt sad that a few children had died, he rejoiced because God had shown him the radio program that had saved many of them.

"Ramon," the elders decided several days later, "we are so grateful for your help in saving our children that we will allow you to move to Pandurukan. You may leave whenever you like."

Ramon was too excited to do anything but smile in reply. That day he and Dulion began packing their things. Ramon sang as he worked. They were finally moving!

Thank You, Panginoon, he thought joyfully. *Thank You for hearing my prayers. Life will be perfect from now on.*

But on the day when Ramon was going to move to Pandurukan, something terrible happened. Three more children in his village died unexpectedly. Ramon was devastated.

"Ah," the elders told him, "this is a very bad omen. You should not be moving."

However, they did not insist that he stay. And Ramon and Dulion set out for Pandurukan, bittersweet joy in their hearts.

Two weeks later Ramon was baptized in a stream near the Anni River. His journey was finished. Or was it?

(to be continued)

1. What do you think Ramon's dream meant?
2. Why did Ramon want to be close to the light in his dream?
3. Why do you think God waited to heal Dulion until after the elders had tried their ways and after Ramon had stopped reading the Bible and then started again?
4. How do you think God will use Ramon in the next story?

One of your friends fell down in a bicycling accident and is now in the hospital. The doctors tell you that he will be paralyzed from the waist down. You and some of your classmates decide to hold an all-night prayer vigil for him in the chapel at the hospital.

After a long, sleepless night, you tiptoe into his room the next morning. Has God answered your prayers? You hold your breath and wait for good news.

"Nothing's changed," your friend tells you with tears in his eyes. "I still can't move my legs. The prayers didn't work."

What will you do?

Read John 4:21-24. Even though the place is not the most important factor when it comes to worshiping God, some places do hold special spiritual significance. Find a special place in your house or outdoors where you want to have worship for a week, and stick to your plan. Notice how a consistent location affects your worship time.

Alone or with your family, try building an altar to the Lord. You can use it to praise Him, to offer a special request, to ask forgiveness, or to give thanks for a particular blessing. See if you can find several examples of the usage of altars in the Old Testament to help you.

Ramon preaches a sermon for church.

What's happening: Ramon has another dream about God. He retrieves his Bible and begins praying for Dulion's healing again. After he builds an altar and prays very earnestly, Dulion is healed. Ramon begins listening to the radio at night, and one night he hears of natural medical remedies. The next day children in the village get sick, and Ramon cures them. In gratitude, the elders let Ramon and his family move to Pandurukan. Ramon is baptized as a Seventh-day Adventist Christian.

* * *

Ramon loved to go to church. He continued to read his Bible, and when the missionary was gone, he took over the village worship services, sharing with the people the precious truths he had learned.

One night when Ramon was away from Pandurukan, he felt uneasy about his wife. He felt that she was in great danger. He dropped to his knees and pleaded for her safety, then went to sleep.

While he slept, he dreamed he was standing on a

mountain overlooking the village of Pandurukan and its valley. Thousands upon thousands of angels surrounded the village. So many angels lined the mountains around the valley that they looked like brilliant white clouds covering everything except for a hole in the center. He awoke and thanked God for this evidence of His protection. When he returned to Pandurukan, he found Dulion unharmed.

As months went by, a growing conviction came to Ramon that he needed to pray for the people in his former village. Daily he poured out his heart to God in intercessory prayer for them.

"Panginoon," he pleaded each night, "please help them to move to Pandurukan so they can learn about You and find freedom from the spirits. I want them to know about the love I have found in You."

Over the months Ramon often traveled back to his village, sharing with them, encouraging them, and pleading and praying with them to move. Most of them were willing, but several skeptics refused.

"The day you moved, three children died," the elders reminded him. "That was a very bad omen. If the spirits do not want us to move, we will stay here."

But Ramon was not discouraged. "God has answered many of my prayers. He will not fail me now."

All the elders eventually agreed to the move. But one little wrinkled, stoop-shouldered, elderly woman stubbornly refused, so the rest of them agreed to stay for her.

Not long after this, Ramon had yet another dream. He was standing beside a deep, jagged chasm. It was so deep that the bottom was shrouded in blackness, but he could faintly see a fast-moving river flowing at the bottom. Hundreds of Alangans stood with him, crying and wailing that the end of the world had come.

Behind them was blackness. In front of them, on the other side of the canyon, was brilliant light. Many Alangans dropped to their knees and pleaded with tears and groaning for Ramon to help them get to the other side—to safety.

Ramon turned and walked back into the darkness to where a huge tree was growing. Taking out his machete, he attacked the tree at its base, hacking out huge chips of wood as he chopped. Beads of sweat stood out on his forehead, and his breath became labored as he fought on at a furious pace.

At last the giant tree quivered, swayed, and crashed to the earth. Quickly Ramon chopped the limbs off and, panting and struggling, dragged the tree to the lip of the chasm. As he stood catching his breath, the Alangans continued crying and wailing but didn't come to help him. After a brief rest, with superhuman effort, he managed to push the large tree across the canyon to the other side. He had built a bridge.

Immediately Ramon jumped up onto the log, bounced up and down to test that it was solid, and then walked across to the far side of the chasm. Joyfully he turned around and beckoned, calling out for the Alangans to follow him over to the light. At that instant Ramon awoke, not knowing if any had followed.

Over the past several years this dream has been repeated many times. Ramon knows that God is asking him to work for his fellow Alangans and to show them Jesus and the way to eternal life. This was God's purpose long ago when He first gave Ramon the desire to learn to read the Bible. God had been preparing him for this great task, allowing sickness, circumstances, and trials to mold and shape and nurture his faith.

The old woman from Ramon's former village died not long after this dream. The elders agreed to the move, and Ramon escorted the entire village to their new home in Pandurukan.

Within two years, with the help of the missionaries, he saw almost all of his neighbors from his former village baptized, including many of the elders who had insisted he stop reading the Bible and praying. God in His infinite love had answered all of Ramon's prayers.

1. What did the tree represent in Ramon's dream?
2. What did the other side of the canyon represent?
3. Why did Ramon have to work so hard to chop down the tree?
4. Read Psalm 34:7. What kind of danger could Dulion have faced when Ramon felt impressed to pray for her safety?
5. Has God ever talked to you in a dream? Why do you think He communicates to some people through dreams and not to others?

Scenario

Your dad's side of the family doesn't believe in God. When you get together at Christmas, there are always a few arguments between your family and the rest of the clan. You're usually excluded from these discussions.

But one day you overhear your uncle Louie talking with his wife. "Christmas would be the perfect holiday if we took Christ out of it," he says sarcastically. "I wish some people could see the truth in that."

You're sure Uncle Louie knows you're in the room, and you feel that you should respond to his comment. *What should you say?*

Take Action!

Are there any members of your family who have not accepted Jesus yet? How about any of your friends? Do you, like Ramon, feel a responsibility to help your entire town find eternal life? Think about whom God might be calling you to witness to, and reach out to that person or group with His love.

The people in Ramon's village were willing to move their entire town to be closer to the missionaries and the gospel. Are you willing to make any major changes in your life for God? Think of at least one way you can draw closer to God by making a change, and put the change into action.

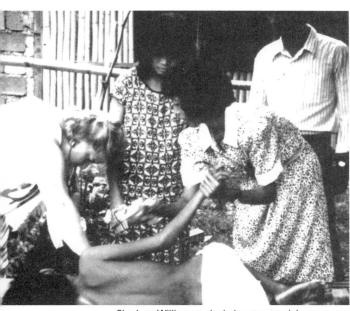

Charleen Williams and a helper treat a sick young man.

43

"Pastor Williams!"

Howard Williams heard the hoarse whisper, but thought he was imagining it. He was, after all, in the middle of church! He adjusted his position on the rough wooden pew and stared intently toward the front of the building.

"Pastor Williams!"

Again the insistent whisper caught his attention. This time several people stared in his direction. Realizing the voice was actually real, Howard turned toward the window and met the anxious gaze of a Mangyan villager.

"Go to Charleen at once!" the villager whispered. "She has an emergency patient!"

Howard's heart began pounding loudly inside his chest. What could be wrong this time? He had arrived at church late because of several unplanned medical visits, and now this!

Howard quietly slid from his seat and hurried home. He found Charleen busily working on a 12-year-old boy who lay unconscious on a makeshift stretcher.

"What's wrong with him?" Howard asked, reaching down to touch the boy's forehead. "He's burning up with fever!"

"His family says he's been getting steadily worse for five days," Charleen replied. "They finally carried him five hours on this stretcher to reach our house. We have to get this fever down!"

Charleen and Howard spent the next hour lowering the boy's fever with cold baths. They observed him carefully, trying to decide what his sickness might be. The boy's worried family surrounded them with questions, and Charleen and Howard began to feel stifled.

Before they could escape to eat a much-needed lunch, an elderly woman grabbed Howard by the shirtsleeve. "Please, Pastor." She looked hopefully up at him, her wrinkled face contorted in pain. "My tooth, it hurts!"

"Oh, that's right!" Howard slapped his forehead. "This woman's been asking me to remove her rotten tooth all morning." Standing beside him, the woman grinned, revealing a black tooth near the side of her smile.

Charleen sighed. She had felt sick earlier that day, and Howard could tell that stress was taking its toll.

"I'll tell you what." He turned back to the waiting woman. "My wife and I will give you some rice to cook for lunch, and after lunch I'll pull your tooth."

"Thank you, Pastor! Thank you!" Despite her pain, the old woman smiled even more widely and followed Howard into the house to receive her rice.

When the door finally shut behind the woman, Charleen heaved another huge sigh of fatigue. "I don't know how much longer I can go on," she confessed to Howard, "but I don't want to leave that little boy untreated."

Howard nodded and reached for the pot of cooked rice. He heaped a spoonful onto Charleen's plate. "I'm still not sure what's wrong with him," he said slowly. "Could it be malaria?" He gazed out the window at the boy, now conscious, as he tossed on his stretcher. The boy's family huddled around him, afraid and confused. Every now and then the boy muttered a few unintelligible words and slipped into a half-conscious state.

"I have a feeling it's cerebral malaria," Charleen offered. "He's acting pretty loony, don't you think?"

Howard nodded, then bowed his head and silently prayed for his lunch and the medical patients in his front yard. *Please, Lord, give us wisdom,* he pleaded sincerely. *Teach us how to reach these people.*

After lunch Howard approached the woman he'd spoken with earlier. "Are you ready?"

Spry for her obvious age, the woman leaped to her feet. "Let's go!"

Howard asked the woman to sit down in his makeshift dentist's chair. "Open your mouth as wide as you can. This tooth will be out in no time," he promised as he administered the anesthetic. After just a few minutes he removed the offending tooth with hardly any effort.

"That's it!" he called to the woman. "You can close your mouth if you want to. Be careful of the gauze—that's to stop the bleeding."

The woman closed her mouth, stood to her feet, and beamed up at Howard like a pleased child.

"Salamat po, Pastor! ["Thank you, Pastor!"]" she said simply, her gauze-filled grin widening each second. *"Salamat po.* It has hurt so long. Sometimes I could not work or even sleep." The woman's eyes filled with gratitude and, had she been an American, Howard felt sure she would have thrown her arms around him in a huge bear hug.

"You're very welcome," Howard replied. A grin of his own spread quickly across his face as his own heart filled with joy. "It shouldn't hurt anymore now."

The woman looked up at Howard, one hand holding her still-numb jaw. "I'm so glad you pulled it out. I want to pay you."

"Oh, you don't have to do that! I just wanted to help you out."

But the wrinkled old woman had already turned to her betel nut pouch. She pulled out two coins, which were equivalent to three and a half cents in the United States.

This must be all the money she has, Howard realized with a start. *This has to be a tremendous sacrifice for her!* He fought back the tears as he wordlessly accepted the money. He couldn't turn it down when she'd given it so freely. *We are the hands of Jesus Christ to these people,* Howard thought as he watched the old woman walk away. *I believe in this type of mission work with all my heart!*

Still marveling at his experience, Howard approached Charleen at the sick boy's stretcher.

"He doesn't seem much better," Charleen told him softly. "I think our guess is correct." The boy suddenly let loose a stream of words that made no sense in either Tagalog (national language of the Philippines) or English. His family turned helplessly to Howard and Charleen.

"He needs professional help," Charleen whispered to Howard.

Within minutes Howard and Charleen had convinced the boy's family to let them take him to the hospital, an hour and a half's drive away. The doctor on duty confirmed their diagnosis and recommended that the boy remain in the hospital if his family wanted him to live. The family decided he could stay.

Exhausted, Howard and Charleen started the long journey home. It had been a strange Sabbath, filled with highs and lows and incredible sweeping emotions. Tears once again filled Howard's eyes as he related the story of the toothless old woman. "I know this is where we belong," he said quietly to his wife as he reached for her hand. "I know God is using us here in Mindoro."

She silently agreed. Both Howard and Charleen felt the peace of the Holy Spirit envelop them as they drove home in the gathering dusk.

Get Into the Action!

1. How did Howard and Charleen know that the boy in their care had cerebral malaria?
2. Why did the Williamses feel it was all right to treat their patients on the Sabbath? (Hint: the book of Matthew has some good discussions of the Sabbath.)
3. What story does the old woman remind you of? (Read Luke 21:1-4.)

You trudge into the house, tired after a day of standard-ized tests at school. Your mind is a muddle of typed ques-tions and blank ovals waiting to be filled in. Your mom calls a greeting from the kitchen as you head toward your room. You hear your little sister crying in the back bedroom.

That's OK, you think defensively. *Mom will take care of her.* But you know that your mom is busy. Your dad will be home soon, and Mom looks pretty frazzled.

Man! you complain to yourself. *Why do I always have to help out? I'm tired and I just want to relax for a minute!* Your sister's cries grow even louder, but you settle down on your bed and try to shut them out.

What will you do in this situation?

Read the following portion of a letter from Howard Williams. Write a response that you would mail if you had just received this letter yourself.

"It is easy here to see the struggle going on between good and evil. In more affluent societies, unfortunately, somehow we have been lulled into a stupor, oftentimes to the point that we . . . negate the existence of the devil. Satan is going about as a roaring lion seeking whom he can devour. Friends, don't let it be you.

"There is so much to tell and so little space to tell it in, but for now I will close by saying that God is working so many miracles for us here. We know that He is in control. The devil is angered by it, however, and is not content to sit back and do nothing. Please remember us in your prayers, that God will strengthen us and guide us to do His will."

Make a list of your most prized possessions. Place a checkmark by the things you would not give up for a month. Place an "X" beside the things you would not give up for a week. Place a star by the things you would not give up for even one day. Finally, underline the items you would never choose to do without. How many of these things could keep you from a closer relationship with Jesus? Pray for a spirit like the woman who gave everything she had to Jesus.

44

Charleen Williams checks out a tuberculosis patient.

Victories at Danginan By Howard Williams

Sweat poured off their faces as Howard and Charleen Williams crested the hill and started their descent to the chief's cornfield, spread out below them like a rumpled brown-and-green quilt. In Danginan village, now only a couple of shouts away, a drama had already begun that would change the destiny of this tribe of Mangyans forever.

It all began a few weeks earlier when Howard and Charleen had started visiting the village bimonthly to treat the sick. At first the villagers had received them coldly and with suspicion. But after a few of the Mangyans recovered quickly from their ailments, some of them decided they could trust the newcomers.

Not all, however, were ready to accept a foreigner's medicine. One woman suffered a week of pain and fever from a large abscess on her thigh before agreeing to call the Williamses for help. It was for this call that Howard and Charleen had trekked to Danginan village that day.

Upon reaching the village Howard and Charleen

received a noisy welcome from the dogs, but didn't see many people around.

"Hello!" Howard called into the silence. "Is anybody here today? Helloooo, helloooooo!"

Finally a woman emerged from a dark hut and agreed to lead them to the sick woman in the village. She silently led them to the farthest hut in the village. There they discovered the woman lying in a corner, covered by a thin and filthy blanket. Beads of sweat stood out on her nose and forehead from pain and fever.

Charleen pulled back the blanket to expose her leg. It was inflamed from knee to groin with the worst abscess either of them had ever seen. The smell from the wound nearly sent Howard to the door, but he ignored his nose and concentrated on the woman. A homemade herbal plaster covered the abscess and hid it from view.

"What will you do?" the woman's husband asked them from across the room, afraid to get too close to the strange White people.

"First of all, we'll clean the wound," Charleen told him. "Please begin heating some water."

After cleaning, draining, and bandaging the wound, Howard and Charleen left for home. The woman already felt better, and they knew she'd make a speedy recovery. "We'll be back tomorrow to help you change your bandages."

Within a week the woman's wound had noticeably cleared, and her ready smile spoke of how medical missionary work can break down barriers. Before long she began walking and performing everyday chores once again. Her family was noticeably pleased. Howard, Charleen, and Aaron (a student missionary staying with them) thought this was the end of the story. They were wrong.

One Friday evening just before dark a Mangyan came to Howard and Charleen's gate, carrying his oldest brother, Junior, across his shoulders.

"Can you treat him?" the Mangyan asked Howard. He explained that he had seen what was happening in the village, and Howard understood that the man trusted them. A few years earlier another of his brothers had become sick and had been taken to the medicine man for treatment. But the brother died.

"Now," explained the man as he laid his brother on the ground beside him, "I have been hiking since before dawn to bring my brother to you."

After checking Junior over, Howard and Charleen knew for sure that he had advanced tuberculosis and was very malnourished. However, after only a few days of treatment, good food, and bathing he began to feel stronger. He stayed camped in the Williamses' backyard until he made a full recovery.

Another day at about noon three Mangyan men arrived at Howard and Charleen's house with a request. "Please come with us to Danginan," they asked politely. "We have brought a patient from Sibaroi, a village back in the hills. He is too sick to bring him here." Of course Howard and Charleen agreed to go with them.

Binlin, the patient in question, was in the last stages of tuberculosis and wracked by amoebic dysentery.

"Can we help him at all?" Charleen asked Howard doubtfully. "He looks pretty bad."

Howard shrugged and glanced at Binlin's waiting family. "We'd better try." Binlin's family had attempted every cure they could think of—a month in the hospital and, when that didn't work, treatment by a medicine man. The medicine man had told them to kill three pigs and have a feast in order to heal Binlin. Of course it didn't help. Over the next three months Binlin had wasted away to skin and bones. Now the family gazed expectantly at Howard and Charleen, their last ray of hope for Binlin's recovery.

Charleen immediately administered medicine for Binlin's sickness. "Here," she began, thrusting the remainder of the medicine at Binlin's brother. "Give this to him every day, and come by our house tomorrow for more supplies." The frightened man nodded and promised to show up.

"We'll be back to check on Binlin this Sabbath," she promised as they left the village near sunset. "We expect to see improvement in his condition."

But when they returned in several days, Binlin showed no general improvement. On the contrary, he could now speak only in a faint whisper. Binlin's brother shrugged. "We forgot to give him the tuberculosis medicine and vitamins," he said in a flat, emotionless voice.

Howard was alarmed. *What should I do?* he wondered desperately. *This case is way out of my league.*

He longed to pray for the suffering man, but did he dare mention his God to the people? Just six weeks earlier the Mangyan elders had clearly stated that they didn't want the Williamses' religion. Howard began to sweat as he looked around the crowd of worried faces at Binlin's bedside.

If I do pray for the man and he dies, what will they think of my God? he asked himself silently. *On the other hand, if God chose to restore him to health, what a testimony it would be.* Howard's faith wavered because he knew an unseen battle was raging over Binlin and his people. He discussed the matter with his interpreter and with Aaron.

"The villagers see that their medicine won't be enough to cure him," Howard's interpreter explained. "They are willing to let you pray."

Howard knelt and poured out his heart to God on the people's behalf. After concluding his prayer and telling a few stories of answered prayers in his own life, Howard headed for home.

"There's nothing more I can do," he confided to Aaron as they walked through the jungle. "I've told them to continue his medication and to feed him healthy foods. The rest is up to them . . . and God.

Later, after a trip to Manila, Howard learned what had happened. When Charleen went to Danginan to check on Binlin, she found him much more alert and able to talk again. The family was pleased and requested that Howard return to pray for him again. Gone were the suspicious faces and fearful expressions. Gone were the turned backs and angry comments. The chief even suggested that the villagers build a small house so that Howard and Charleen could rest in it when they visited.

Needless to say, Howard and Charleen were thrilled. "Not only are they accepting us," Howard rejoiced to his wife, "but they are also opening up to our God! What more could we ask for?"

Howard smiled contentedly. It had been another eventful week, and he was glad the commotion had slowed down for a while. Already he and Charleen had spent hours poring over medical books and jungle remedy manuals.

But, he decided as he settled into his chair on the porch, *it's all worth it for the goal of introducing Christ to the Mangyans.* He knew more trials would come, but for now he was grateful for God's obvious leading in their relationship with the people of Danginan.

Get Into the Action!

1. Why were the villagers of Danginan so suspicious of Howard, Charleen, and Aaron in the beginning?
2. What experience began to change their minds?
3. Why were they willing to let Howard pray for Binlin later on?

Scenario

You have just started school in a new neighborhood, and you can already tell that it's going to be a tough year. Evidently your religious reputation has preceded you. Kids actually seem afraid to talk with you! It's as though you have a sign on your back that says "Ignore Me." You don't know how much longer you can take the isolation, but you can't force the kids to be friendly.

What will you do?

Take Action!

Read Matthew 10:16. How did Howard, Charleen, and Aaron follow this advice? How can you follow it when you are dealing with non-Christian people?

Make a list of the kinds of people you have a hard time loving or are afraid of. How can you show your love and friendship to them? How can you learn to understand them better? Focus on becoming more loving and compassionate toward them.

Mar and Ching Amurao and their daughter, Marconelle.

Mar's Miracle By Mr. Mar Amurao

Mar Amurao clenched his jaw and stared out the rain-streaked windshield. In front of him the muddy road rose almost straight up into the mountains of Mindoro. He pressed his foot on the accelerator, and the jeep's engine roared—but the vehicle refused to budge.

"We're stuck, aren't we?" Ching, Mar's wife, asked beside him. "What are we going to do?"

Mar felt like crying. Every aspect of this trip to Sablayan to work with the Williamses seemed to be failing. After far too many delays they had finally transported the jeep by boat to the island of Mindoro. Unfortunately, they were on the opposite side from the Williamses! Just as they had begun to drive over the mountains to reach them, heavy rains had set in. And now this! Already several boys had come along to help, but nothing could move the obstinate jeep.

Mar leaned his head on the steering wheel. "I don't know," he admitted quietly. "I don't know what to do."

Suddenly Ching's body stiffened. "Look," she whispered carefully. "Soldiers."

Mar's head snapped up. It was true! Two men with guns and bullets slung across their shoulders slogged down the mountain toward them. They waved at the jeep—but were they friendly?

Before Mar could react, one of the soldiers spoke.

"Hello!" the soldier called out, yelling to be heard above the pounding storm. "Don't be afraid! Is your jeep stuck?"

Thank You, Lord, Mar thought in relief. "It sure is! Can you help us?"

"Of course, of course." The first soldier swung his gun behind his back and put his shoulder into the rear bumper of the jeep. After a few united efforts the two men finally pushed the vehicle out.

"Thank you!" Mar leaned out of the window and waved at the two men.

The first soldier approached the window, a worried look on his face. "We were happy to help you," he began, "but we think you'd better not continue tonight. The rains will probably turn into a monsoon. The roads will not be safe."

"But we have no shelter!"

The soldier motioned with his gun. "Back a little ways," he volunteered, "is a big house where you can stay until the storm is over."

Grateful for their advice, Mar turned the jeep around and inched down the road toward the house.

"Welcome!" A wrinkled elderly woman opened the door to Mar's knock. "You must be stuck on the road. You'll stay with us until the storm is over."

Mar and Ching nodded silently and smiled at a younger man seated on the floor. Against the wall were stacks of rice, corn, and other food reserved for the rainy season. Ching had noticed mangoes that had fallen off the trees because of the storm.

"We will be well fed here," she whispered to her husband as the woman escorted them into her spacious house.

He grinned and pointed to heaven. "Thanks to God, I have a feeling we'll be treated like their own relatives!"

Mar and Ching's predictions came true. For at least a week

the family housed and fed them without complaint. "You cannot leave until the rains stop," they insisted again and again. "It's still not safe to travel."

During the week Mar and Ching taught the generous family about praying before eating and shared with them the story of salvation. Then they taught them how to make some good food out of banana blossoms and how to preserve the mango fruit that had been blown to the ground by the typhoon. Mar and Ching even taught them about personal hygiene.

The family, in turn, showed Mar and Ching how to plant rice the "native" way and allowed them to help with the planting process. Finally, after seven rainy days had passed, the family agreed let them go.

"We will miss you," the old woman said tearfully. "We have enjoyed your worships and prayers."

Other villagers and family members joined in her sadness. "Thank you for staying with us. Please come back soon!"

Mar and Ching started their journey again. The road had dried somewhat, and eight villagers and a carabao had been sent to help them over the rough spots. However, after three successful hours of travel, the jeep again refused to cooperate. A terrible smell came from under the hood, and strange noises told Mar that the clutch was slipping. The jeep could no longer move on its own.

The carabao was getting tired and cranky as it pulled. Suddenly its yoke gave way like a spring and hit the windshield in front of Mar's face. Miraculously, no one was hurt. They paused to thank God for His wonderful care.

But now they were stranded a second time, this time in a less friendly village. Luckily someone agreed to house Mar and Ching for the night. The next day, which was Mar's birthday, began at 4:00 in the morning. Mar set out early, hiking toward the city of San Jose in search of a bulldozer to pull the jeep.

As he walked along, Mar poured out his heart to God. *Oh, Lord,* he prayed, *I ask only one thing for my birthday. Please help us to get out of this dangerous area. Thank You, Father.*

Assured of God's protection, Mar hiked into San Jose in a

better mood. However, he soon found that a bulldozer would cost more than 1 million pesos (US$50,000), not including the driver and any other expenses. Undaunted, he decided to try to fix the jeep himself. He found a ride back to the base of the mountain and began the long trek toward the jeep.

As he trudged through the mud, Mar again wondered what God had in mind for this trip. He just wanted to find a warm bed to lie down in, and he could only imagine his wife's discomfort!

Suddenly Mar stopped dead in his tracks. What was that noise? He hoped it was a truck that could take him the rest of the way.

The sound grew louder, and Mar's spirits began to revive. He wouldn't have to hike all the way back to the jeep after all! Soon Mar recognized the deep-throated motor of . . . a bulldozer? *Why would a bulldozer be traveling this way?* he wondered fleetingly.

And then the bulldozer lumbered around a corner, and Mar wondered no more. He spotted their tiny muddy jeep bumping along behind it with Ching and all their supplies.

"You are God's gift for my birthday!" Mar yelled up at the puzzled bulldozer operator, tears flowing from his eyes. He thanked God for a wonderful birthday present.

1. Why do you think there were so many delays in their trip?
2. What kind of impact do you think Mar and Ching had on the villagers they stayed with?

You stare out the window of your family's station wagon. Wide fields of some strange plant pass before your eyes as the car speeds around yet another curving corner. Your dad, at the wheel, seems tense and nervous. Your mom isn't saying much of anything. And you and your brother have just gotten in another fight, so you aren't speaking either.

Once again your family has gotten lost on your annual vacation to the country. But this time you've been lost for an entire afternoon!

How can you brighten the situation?

Think of an instance when things did not go the way you expected them to. Now make a list of the blessings that you received from that experience.

How can you provide a special birthday blessing for someone else? Plan a special party, make a card, or think of some other way to make a person's special day even better.

Mar's Miracle • Beyond the Edge

From a Saul to a Paul By Tim Holbrook

Brother Gimeno and Tim Holbrook

Beads of sweat trickled down the pastor's glistening red face as he clenched his fists in fear and anger. Every muscle tensed in his body; every nerve alert and screaming. He hardly dared to breathe against the feel of the cold point of a submachine gun pressed into his chest.

No one moved. The congregation had formed a line down both sides of the center aisle and looked to their pastor for direction. Should they obey the soldier and do the unthinkable?

The pastor knew the soldier at a glance. This was Commander Bocay, the man whose name struck fear in every Christian's heart. He was the commander and originator of the National People's Army (NPA), a lawless band of soldiers who waged constant warfare on outlying villages and on the government soldiers. Villagers feared Commander Bocay for his countless acts of violence. It was rumored that he had killed at least 281 people, and the pastor did not want to be number 282.

Slowly, reluctantly, the pastor started walking, gingerly stepping on all the congregation's Bibles that had been placed down the center of the aisle. The church members followed, one by one, urged on by the gun-waving soldier. Once out the door, the people ran for their lives, fear stabbing at their hearts.

Commander Bocay watched them flee with a smirk on his face. These Christians were all the same. When it came down to saving their own skin, they would do anything to live. He idly wondered why Christians irritated him so much. He'd never been a religious man. God was for the weak-willed, simple people who needed a crutch to deal with life. He, on the other hand, had pride and ability. He didn't need anything or anyone. He was invincible. A satisfied smile crossed his hardened face. He remembered all the times he had been in gunfights, bullets whizzing and whining by his head while he remained unharmed. *A person should have faith in himself and nothing else,* Commander Bocay reminded himself again as he watched the last of the congregation filing out on top of the Bibles.

Suddenly his sharp ears detected a noise in the sanctuary. Quiet sobs. Curious, he strode toward the sound. There, crouched down under a pew, was a sunbaked old woman in a tattered dress. Her thin arms hugged a Bible to her chest while she rocked back and forth, sobbing bitterly. A stream of tears coursed down her wrinkled old face.

"Why don't you walk down the aisle like everyone else, old woman?" the commander asked mockingly. "None of them had any problems walking."

But the little grandmother refused to move, still clutching her Bible while the tears continued to flow.

"Woman, if you don't walk, I'll kill you," said Bocay coldly as he planted the muzzle of the machine gun on her chest.

Still she refused, eyes closed, her arms across her chest, her Bible pressed close.

Commander Bocay pulled the trigger.

* * *

Brother Gimeno, as Commander Bocay now preferred to be called, leaned back and closed his eyes. Tim Holbrook had been listening intently to his incredible conversion story.

"I was arrogant and full of pride then," Brother Gimeno said, opening his eyes at last. "I needed no one. I could do it all myself. I thought nothing of killing. I have killed 282 people. See? I have the number tattooed on my thigh." He pulled up his pant leg to show Tim. Then he sat back and related the rest of his story.

He was captured in 1972 by government forces and sentenced to death by a firing squad. He and two other men were led out to a field and commanded to stand with their backs to a freshly dug ditch. The soldiers raised their guns.

Gimeno was desperate. This was the only time in his life he had needed anyone else. His parents were nominal Catholics, so he was somewhat familiar with the saints. "Help me, Saint Peter, help me, Saint Paul. Please help me, Mother Mary!" he called into the sky.

A shot rang out, and the man on his left fell. Another shot, and the man on his right fell. He waited, the sweat beading on his forehead, his breath stopped, and his eyes clenched tightly shut. But no shot came. Instead, his captors led him to an interrogation room and grilled him for hours. Gimeno answered yes to every question because he was told he would be killed if he lied.

Despite his honesty, Gimeno was then sentenced to death by the electric chair. They strapped him down and left him, saying it would be over in two minutes. First, they would try to patch a radio message through to President Marcos. Two minutes later Marcos radioed back and commuted his sentence to life in prison in exchange for testifying against the leaders of the NPA.

Gimeno's captors placed him in a cell that was so small he couldn't lie down or stand up. It was dark and dank, and for six months he had no clothes, blankets, or netting to allay the swarms of mosquitoes in the cell. Gimeno remained there for three years.

One Saturday, five years later, as Gimeno lay on his bunk in a new cell and wondered what was left of his life, a pretty melody floated past his ears. *That's beautiful,* he thought idly. Since he had nothing else to do, he walked out into the prison yard and joined the church service in progress.

The song, "Face to Face," moved Gimeno like no other song had. He became interested in the sermon, and when the preacher offered to study the Bible with him, he accepted.

"By this time, I believed that someone had saved me for a reason," Brother Gimeno said. "I was saved from all the bullets during my fighting, from the firing squad, and from the electric chair. I knew I couldn't save myself."

The pastor continued to study with Gimeno during the following months, and in 1976 he was baptized into the Adventist Church.

"Now my pride is gone," Brother Gimeno told Tim. "I am alive only by the grace of God. He humbled me, and now He has a purpose for me." Brother Gimeno paused, emotion working in his face. "In 1992 I was released under Corazon Aquino's amnesty program after spending 20 years in prison."

Today Brother Gimeno is part of the 1,000 Missionary Movement in Mindoro, working with prison ministries. He tirelessly holds services in all the surrounding jails, often with the help of some literature evangelists. He has now won more than 300 souls for Christ and has many more ready for baptism. Brother Gimeno truly is a Saul who turned into a Paul.

Get Into the Action!

1. Why did Brother Gimeno (Commander Bocay) dislike Christians so much?
2. Why do you think the old grandmother would not leave the church?
3. How is Brother Gimeno's story like the story of Saul, who later became Paul? (Look up the story for yourself in the book of Acts.)
4. How do you think the Christians in the Philippines felt when they heard that Gimeno had been saved?

Tony, the school bully, approaches you with a grin on his pimply face. You try to avoid him, but he's headed straight for you and you don't have time to duck into a classroom. "Hi," Tony says sheepishly. "Can I talk to you for a minute?" Your mind flashes back to several years ago when you first met Tony. He'd grabbed your lunch box and eaten its contents in front of you. He'd continued this ritual for several weeks before a teacher finally caught him. And that was just the beginning of your encounters with Tony. He'd cheated on you in recess, told lies about you to get you in trouble, "borrowed" your things and never returned them—the list seemed endless. And now he wanted to talk to you? *Forget it!* your mind screams, but your mouth refuses to work. Before you can answer, Tony jumps into his story. "I met a preacher," he tells you, "and I'm converted now! I'm so happy! I just thought you might understand."

You freeze. Is this another trick? Tony's never told you the truth in his life. Your mind reels, trying to decide how to react. *What will you do?*

1. Read 2 Corinthians 5:17. How are you a new creation because you know Jesus? Ask your parents the same question.

2. Write out 2 Corinthians 5:17 on several 3" x 5" cards. Give a card to each new baptized member of your church. Be sure to write a personal, handwritten note on the back of each card and include the date of each person's baptism.

3. Ask your Sabbath school teacher or schoolteacher about visiting or witnessing to inmates in a prison. Remember to discuss safety issues first. As a class, decide on an outreach project for the inmates.

This young man plays the kudlungan, *a traditional Palawano instrument*

Palawan, home of the Muslim Palawano, Molbog, and Jama Mapun people, is a long isolated island in the southwestern Philippines.

Scattered settlements and shifting agriculture predominate, with rice as the main food crop. Corn, coconuts, beans, and sweet potatoes are also grown by the Palawano people.

Manila

Philippines

Palawan

Palawan, Philippines

Timothy George tries out some Palawano stilts. Ouch!

Timothy's World By Timothy George

Hi! My name's Timothy, and I'm 10 years old. Since some of you might wonder what we do here in Palawan, I thought I'd write you a description.

Sometimes we hike into the mountains. If the trail is too wet and slippery, I end up doing a lot of traveling on my bottom. The first part and the last part are very steep, and part of it is up a river. Usually we see snakes or birds. This last time we saw a cobra. We also saw some yellow leeches and some black ones, too. They look like long slimy tapeworms.

I like school, but it's home school. When it gets too hot, we go and play in the ocean. It's a quarter mile away. Or we swim in the Tamlang River, where you can see clear to the bottom.

I miss some things about the States, but mainly I miss all the food. I miss pizza and haystacks and apples, oranges, pears, and grapefruits. I used to have grapefruit every morning, but now I always eat rice for breakfast. I miss peaches and strawberries, too. We have two buckets of dried peaches, but they aren't as good as peaches picked straight off the tree.

We have a cat named Nimrod. He is black and white and has a tail. That might sound funny, but most cats here don't have much of a tail or they are just short, crooked tails.

We don't climb trees very much because most of the trees are banana trees or coconut trees. You can't climb banana trees because they are not made out of wood. They're made mostly of water and would probably fall over, because they aren't very strong. Also, if you puncture the tree, the water will run out, and if it gets on you, it will turn your clothes red.

You can't climb coconut trees because they're too tall and they don't have branches. The people here can climb them, but we can't because it is too hard. The people here cut little slits in the trees and then they wiggle their toes into each slit and climb up the tree. My toes aren't strong enough to do that.

Oh, yes, I also miss the cars and the roads in America. Since the cars and roads here are so terrible, our jeep keeps falling apart. The other day it caught on fire, and we were all sad because it didn't burn up completely. All the grown-ups call it a death trap.

A while ago it rained all day long and washed the bridge away. It also washed a lot of the road away. People don't worry about fixing the bridge during the dry season, but they work a whole lot on it after it washes away. It's fun driving through the river with the jeep. So far we haven't gotten stuck, but sometimes jeepneys and trucks get stuck in the river. Everyone enjoys it a lot and has a good time.

Swimming in the ocean is one of Timothy's favorite activities.

There are always new treasures to find in the Philippines.

It is really fun to watch them getting stuck.

The villagers up in the mountains make stilts that aren't like our stilts at all. They just use two sticks with two little slits on each side of the stick, and then they put the stick between the big toe and the next toe. It gave me a terrible blister between my toes and spread my toes so far apart I thought they would break off. But it doesn't hurt the people up there one bit. Their toes are so far apart it is hard for them to wear shoes. They could carry golf balls between their toes with no problem at all.

The villagers have an open market, and it smells really bad. But that market is where we get our food. I bought 100 pieces of candy there, and it cost 40 pesos. They have all kinds of fish, all sizes and colors, and they have octopuses, squids, sharks, and clams. They eat just about everything that comes out of the ocean. They also have lots of pigs here, very big pigs. Some are at least two feet tall and very fat. They have lots of little piglets, too. Some are pink, and some are black. They like to grunt and squeal, but they usually squeal the most when someone wants to eat them.

Well, that's about all I can think of. Tell me all the interesting things that are happening there. I'd like it if you could come visit. We have cockroaches that are almost three inches long, but the cat eats most of them. We have geckos on the ceiling and spiders in the corners. Every now and then we find a scorpion, but only Mama has gotten stung by one. So come visit soon.

From Timothy George

Get Into the Action!

1. What new things did you learn about the Philippines from Timothy's description?
2. What things would you especially enjoy about Timothy's home? What things would you not enjoy?
3. How do you think Timothy can be a missionary in the Philippines even though he's only 10 years old?

Scenario

You have a pen pal who lives in India and has never been to the United States. Your pen pal wants to know what your country is like and what activities you especially enjoy. You know this is a chance to talk about yourself and a chance to tell your pen pal about God. *How will you respond to your pen pal's request?*

Take Action!

Read and memorize 1 Timothy 4:12.

Spend some time with a young child (age 2-6). Try to see how the child views his or her world. Ask questions about God. Be willing to accept the fact that you might learn some things from the child, and not just the other way around.

Next time you have an idea and are afraid to say it in a group of adults, speak up!

48

Taya, Healing of Body and Soul
By Leonda George

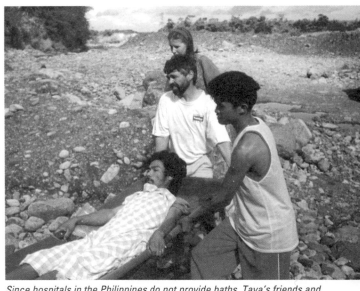

Since hospitals in the Philippines do not provide baths, Taya's friends and family help him bathe in the river.

The adventure began the moment Leonda George spotted Taya lying in the back of the mission jeep. His family, in desperation, had carried him out of the mountains for help. There he lay, a pile of skin and bones, his yellow eyes staring pitifully up at Leonda. She could only hope it wasn't too late to save him.

Leonda knew that Taya's hepatitis had advanced far beyond her experience, so she and her husband, Kent, drove him to the hospital in Brooke's Point. Once they had him settled in, they gathered around and prayed with him.

But this was merely the beginning of Leonda's experience with Taya. His teenage son and nephews, who had brought him out of the mountains, needed someone to provide their meals. Leonda cooked and took food over to the hospital for the family.

Over the next several days Leonda spent much of her time at the hospital giving reassurance and letting the hospital staff know that she was serious about the care the patient received. Several times Taya's nephew radioed her and Kent to come immediately. They would rush to the hospital in the middle of the night, often finding Taya struggling for breath and in serious pain. Many times they were afraid they were losing him. And when it became evident that Taya needed surgery to remove the obstruction in his bile duct and gallbladder, Kent and Leonda prayed that he would survive the surgery.

During Taya's stay in the hospital, he and his Palawano companions received death threats from an individual because they were Christians. So in addition to the emergency medical calls from Taya's family, Leonda and Kent often received calls in the middle of the night that Taya's companions were afraid of their antagonist. Either Kent or Leonda would get up, travel to the hospital, and sit through the night with the scared Palawanos as they crouched on their beds in fright.

After a week of giving nearly undivided attention to Taya, Leonda complained to Kent one afternoon as they headed home from the hospital. "I feel like I'm neglecting my responsibilities in Kamantian! I know I need to help Taya, but I don't want to ignore an entire village for him!"

However, after praying and discussing the matter, both Kent and Leonda felt that they were doing the right thing. Leonda often asked God, "What are You doing? Is Taya even going to live after all this effort?"

Finally, after three long weeks in the hospital, Taya came to Leonda and Kent's house in Brooke's Point. He weighed only 70 pounds because he hadn't eaten or slept well in the hospital the entire time. Leonda knew it would be a challenge to help him gain enough strength to return to the mountains: more feeding and work.

"But I can't complain," she reminded herself. "It will be so much easier to serve every meal at home now, to everyone at the same time!" Still, doubts pestered her at night. How long would Taya's healing process take? When could she get back to her "real" work?

Then, four weeks to the day after Taya had been admitted to the hospital, Leonda took a few minutes out of meal preparation to sit down and talk with him. She told him about her afternoon and mentioned some of the people she had spoken with in town.

After asking a few polite questions, Taya hung his head. In a voice low with shame, he asked Leonda, "How much do I owe you for your help?"

Leonda shrugged. Different family members had asked her the same question all month. They knew that Taya's medicines, blood transfusions, food, doctor bills, and surgery were not free and had often offered to begin payment on the debt.

In the past Leonda had cheerfully replied that there was no payment. "You do not have a debt with us," she had told them again and again. "This is our gift to you." A relieved smile would pass over the family's faces, and yet later they would ask again.

Again Leonda repeated her answer. "You do not have a debt," she assured Taya firmly. "Think of your time in the hospital as our gift to you."

Taya still looked confused, so Leonda decided to illustrate her point.

"Taya," she said slowly, "you are right that the medicines cost big money. The doctors cost big money. And the operation costs big money. But this experience is like the way it is with our Father God. Because of our many sins, we too had a big debt with God. It was a debt so big that we didn't have the 'money' to pay it off. But because of God's big love for us, He sent Jesus to pay the debt that we could never pay ourselves. Jesus died to take away our sins."

Carefully Leonda went on to explain that because of God's love for Taya, many of their friends had helped them pay his bill. It was all a gift. There was no debt!

Suddenly an understanding smile spread across Taya's face, and he lifted his head. His self-respect restored, he grinned like a schoolboy at the vastness of God's gift.

"Ayad na banar, diki ba ["Isn't that really wonderful?"]?" Leonda asked him.

Taya replied without hesitation, *"Ayad na banar* ["That is wonderful!"]!"

"Now," Leonda laughed as she continued, "if you really want to pay back your debt you will get well and get big and strong!"

Taya laughed with her, but before the moment passed, Leonda had to ask one more important question. The time felt right to voice it, so she began. "Taya, if you would like to, you can follow Jesus and accept His payment for your sin debt."

"I do!" Taya responded immediately, his voice still filled with awe.

Leonda's heart leaped with joy. Other members of the house had gathered to hear the discussion, and now they gathered around Taya and led him in his first prayer to Father God, accepting the payment of Jesus to cover his sins.

O Lord, Leonda prayed as Taya offered his thanks to God beside her, *thank You so much! I know there is much for Taya to learn, but I can see that he understands Your love for him. Thank You, Father, for showing me how my weariness and "distraction" from my duty really had a purpose. I know You planned this perfectly, and it was well worth the effort!*

1. Why do you think Kent and Leonda felt it was all right to spend so much time helping Taya?
2. What about the other villagers?
3. Why was Taya so eager to accept Jesus into his life?

Scenario

Your younger sister has borrowed $20 from you to go Christmas shopping. When you lent her the money, you knew she wouldn't be able to repay it for a while—but it's March, and you still haven't seen a penny! You feel that it's your responsibility to make sure she takes care of her debts. But on the other hand, you know she doesn't have a job or any way to repay the money.

What should you do?

Take Action!

Read Romans 13:8. Think of anyone whom you have been unloving toward in the past week or two, and pay them your "debt" of love.

If someone owes you something, consider canceling their debt.

Palinsin's husband, Kawayanan (left), and church elder, Lunito (right), help her walk home after attending church for the very first time.

49

"Ma'am, would you give me some medicine?" asked a low, quiet voice.

Dawn turned to see a shy round-faced young woman of about 20 standing by the clinic porch. "Sure, Palinsin. What's wrong? Where do you hurt?"

"My back is sore all over. It's hard for me to carry my baskets of *nami* (cassava) home from the mountains, and I am so tired."

Dawn checked Palinsin over but didn't find anything unusual. "Here's some Tylenol for you. Let me know if you still feel bad when I come back next Thursday."

Dawn packed up her medicines and headed down the trail for home. Once a week she came up to Mayba to treat the sick. People frequently complained about soreness and backaches from the strenuous physical labor the Alangan performed in order to get their food.

Over the next several months Dawn treated Palinsin for a variety of ailments—backaches, soreness, tiredness, fever, headaches, and stomachaches. Nothing brought relief. She went with Palinsin to see

Palinsin, radiant from her baptism

the doctor in town, but he reached no concrete diagnosis. Palinsin's health slowly deteriorated. She stopped coming to see Dawn when she visited Mayba with Curtis, a student missionary. Months slipped by.

One day, as Tim, Dawn's husband, drove the missionary jeep by the Arnni bridge, a group of Alangan villagers waved him down. They were carrying a small round-faced woman in a hammock, her legs dangling uselessly over the edge.

"Where are you going?" Tim asked.

"We're taking this woman to see a doctor. Would you help us carry her there? We brought her all the way down from Mayba because she can't walk."

"Sure," Tim replied. He was headed that way to pick up Curtis anyway. "Just bring her into the back of the jeep." With many thanks, the villagers complied.

Later, as the jeep bounced along the potholed road, Tim

glanced into the rearview mirror and saw a pair of frightened eyes staring into his. It was Palinsin!

Before he could ask her any questions, Tim saw Curtis waiting for him by the side of the road. Together they asked the people what doctor lived in the nearby town. It turned out that the group was planning to visit the local witch doctor. "Let's take Palinsin to the doctor in town," Tim and Curtis begged. "Please don't visit the witch doctor."

"No," they replied adamantly. "She's already seen that doctor, and he couldn't help her. The witch doctor is powerful enough to give her a cure."

After exhausting all their arguments, Tim and Curtis offered a short prayer for Palinsin and let the small group go. They trooped away, each holding a corner of the hammock.

Several weeks passed with no news about Palinsin. Tim finally learned that the first witch doctor had been unable to help her, so she had gone to another. Each doctor cost Palinsin and her young husband more money and pigs than they could afford. And still Palinsin remained paralyzed from the waist down.

One day Kawayanan, Palinsin's husband, visited Pandurukan. "Pastor," he began sheepishly, "I want to bring Palinsin here. She wants to see the doctor. Will you go get her in your jeep?"

Tim thought for a minute, watching the man's intent expression. "Kawayanan," he finally spoke, "I want to help Palinsin, but you have to understand that God cannot work with Satan. The witch doctors you visited have power from Satan and his spirits. You cannot ask God to heal your wife and then ask Satan as well! You must choose which power you believe in."

"We have tried the spirit's way." Kawayanan hung his head. "Palinsin is worse. We want to try God's way now."

Tim drove to Mayba with a happy heart. He saw real hope for Palinsin and her husband, both spiritually and physically.

Within a week the doctor discovered that Palinsin had tuberculosis of the spine. Tim, Dawn, and Curtis began a long course of treatment. Palinsin stayed at a friend's house while her sister Daily took care of her. Every morning Dawn brought medicine and food for Palinsin and prayed for her. And every Sabbath the small Alangan church prayed for her healing.

Slowly Palinsin improved. First she discovered a barely noticeable feeling in her foot. Then she could wiggle a toe, then bend a knee. As the months slipped by, she grew strong enough to pull herself upright in her hammock. And one special Sabbath she walked slowly and painfully to church, supported by two friends.

Palinsin showed her sincere interest in God by asking countless questions. When Tim announced a new series of baptismal classes, she requested that they be held in her house so she could listen while she lay in her hammock. "I want to be baptized," she told Tim shyly.

Three times a week for several months the class met by Palinsin's crackling cooking fire and studied God's word. Palinsin soaked it all up like a giant sponge. Daily listened thoughtfully in the background.

On the last study night Tim asked each baptismal candidate when they had accepted Jesus.

"Pastor," Palinsin replied, "after I went to the witch doctors and saw that they could not help me, I wanted to come to Pandurukan and learn about *Panginoon* (God). I know now that He is all-powerful, that He is stronger than all the spirits, and I want to live for Him."

The next Sabbath Palinsin and Daily were baptized with the rest of the class. Palinsin carefully and painfully made her way into the waters of the Arnni River. Slowly the waters closed over her head. Then she came back up into the sunlight and a new life in God. *Panginoon* had taken her illness and turned it into something wonderful!

"And we know that in all things God works for the good of those who love him, who have been called according to his purpose" (Romans 8:28).

1. Why do you think Palinsin didn't come to see Curtis and Dawn after her illness grew worse?
2. Why did Palinsin and her husband try the witch doctors before they turned to the missionaries for help?
3. Read Mark 2:1-12. What does this man's story have in common with Palinsin's experience? What role did each person's friends/family play in their recovery?

"I've stopped smoking," your best friend's mom, Paige, tells you the minute you walk into the house. "And this time it's for good!"

You nod and smile, but don't really believe her. She's been stopping and starting for as long as you have known your best friend. And you're right. Several days later, when you see her reaching for a pack of cigarettes, she refuses to look you in the eye. You feel helpless. You know Paige wants to break her habit, but she just can't seem to do it.

One day, as you pass the kitchen on the way to your best friend's room, you see Paige sitting at the table, crying. An unopened pack of cigarettes sits in front of her. *What can you do to help Paige?*

Have you ever given a Bible study? Pick a topic you feel comfortable with and research it. Then create a short study you would be comfortable sharing with a friend or acquaintance who was curious about the topic. Practice giving the study to your friends or family. Think of other topics you'd like to research as well.

Write out the response you would give if someone told you they wanted to be baptized.

Read over your church's baptismal vows and make sure you understand them.

We Are His Hands By Dawn Spoon

Typical Palawano children. Older siblings often baby-sit younger ones while their parents work.

"L ord, reveal Yourself to these people in a way they will understand," Ray Spoon prayed. Wearily he rose from his knees. It had been a long day—people pressing around, needing this or that. There had been very few moments of rest.

Ray climbed into bed with a heavy heart, thinking of the years he had been here. Were there any listening hearts, or were the people merely coming to get free medicines? Doubtful thoughts chased themselves around in Ray's head as he fell into a fitful sleep.

In his dreams Ray found himself in the presence of God. As God looked tenderly at the careworn missionary, He knew and understood the struggles, temptations, and trials he had been through. God listened patiently as Ray unburdened himself and then with compassion answered, "Go back to your village. Prepare yourself for tomorrow. I will come to your village and reveal Myself to your people."

Ray woke up excited. Would God really show Himself to the people? After all these years of seemingly fruitless labor, would God actually reveal Himself? Would they really know Jesus? God had said so, hadn't He?

But God had said to prepare himself. What should he prepare? Ray glanced around his house. He hadn't straightened it for several days because of all the people needing him. He put several picture books away and was reaching for the broom when there was a low cough at the door.

"Oh, great," Ray said with a groan. "God will be here any time now to reveal Himself to the people. I'm supposed to be getting ready and now there are people at my door."

Forcing a smile, Ray went to see who it was. Piring smiled shyly up at him. "My daughter's malaria is almost gone," she said. "But she still won't eat anything unless it's sweet. Do you have any ripe bananas, papayas, or sweet potatoes you could give me for her?"

Ray nearly sent her away empty-handed. After all, he had more important things to do! Suddenly he thought of Jesus. If Jesus had knocked on his door and asked for food for His sick little one, would he turn Him away?

Without hesitation Ray took his own ripe bananas off the shelf, dug some sweet potatoes from his own garden, and sent Piring on her way with the food. Glancing at the clock, he picked up his broom to continue his cleaning.

Another low cough interrupted his preparation. *Now who could it be?* Ray wondered impatiently. He opened the door to see Miso sitting quietly on the front porch step. His face seemed drawn and serious, unlike his usual buoyant spirit.

After the usual greetings and chitchat Miso spilled out his story. "I started a fire in my new field, and then the wind suddenly changed and swept the fire right into my house. I had no time to get my things out. I only have the shorts I'm wearing. My wife and children are the same. Do you have any clothes we could wear and a blanket we could borrow?" Miso's eyes pleaded for understanding and help.

Ray glanced at his watch. Time was wasting. What if God arrived and he was unprepared? Just as Ray began to tell Miso that he should've built his house farther from his field and that

Ray Spoon with one of his villager friends

Miso's own family should lend him supplies, he remembered a book he had recently read. It emphasized that in everything we do or say we should always ask, "What would Jesus do?"

Ashamed of himself, Ray went inside. Surely there must be something Miso's family could wear. Why, he himself owned five clean shirts, and his wife and children had more than enough clothes as well. He carefully chose something for each person in Miso's family. He also selected a warm blanket from the shelf. He gave them to Miso and sent him back to his family, outfitted with the essentials.

Glancing up at the sky, Ray gave a start. It was almost noon, and he hadn't even prepared his food! What if God should come in time for lunch?

As Ray put a pot of rice on the stove, he thought he heard a child crying. Stepping outside to pick some vegetables for lunch, he almost stepped on Ubit, sitting by the door. Little Ubit held her finger tightly. A drop of blood marked the spot where she had cut herself with a *tukew* (knife). Her tears made little streaks down her dirty cheeks. Obviously, she wanted some medicines and a Band-Aid.

But it's such a little cut, Ray complained to himself. *And if she would only keep clean! Besides,* he reasoned, *I have so much to do to prepare for God. He said he would come today.*

As Ray stepped past Ubit, he thought of the words of Jesus. "Whatever you did to one of the least of these brothers of mine, you did for me."

With new understanding he gently looked at the cut finger. Realizing Ubit needed love more than anything, he tenderly carried her to the water and together they washed away the dirt, dried her hand, and put on the Band-Aid. Before long Ubit was smiling again and jumping up to play.

Again and again that day Ray stopped his preparations to help the villagers. When the sun finally set and the last person left his porch, he sat down with a heavy sigh. Why hadn't God come to reveal Himself as He had said He would? Had God let him down?

As Ray sat there contemplating, the scenes of the day slowly passed before him. He saw Piring, who had received food for her sick daughter, and Miso, who had gone home with a smile because he and his family had clothes to wear and a blanket to sleep under. He saw Ubit, who had received love and a Band-Aid. Then he saw Birat, Lamana, and Bungew. There was Imit and Nislid and all the oth-

A Palawano villager

ers who had passed by his door throughout the day.

God tenderly whispered to Ray in the stillness, "My missionary, I did reveal Myself to your people today. I was there when you gave your own limited food supply to Piring's sick child. I was there when you gave your clothes to Miso and his family and shared your blanket with them. I was there when you took time out of your busy schedule to gently care for Ubit's cut finger. I was there revealing Myself to them—through you."

With greater understanding Ray recalled the words of a song they had sung for worship just that morning.

"We are His hands to touch the world around us.
We are His feet to go where he may lead, and
We are His love burning in the darkness.
We are his love shining in the night."

"Prepare *yourself* for tomorrow. I will come to *your* villages and reveal Myself to *your* people."

1. How did the missionary think Jesus would come to reveal Himself to the people?
2. How did He actually reveal Himself to them?
3. Why do you think the missionary was so kind to the villagers?

You've taken a trip to a big city near your house. You and your parents are walking along a side street when you hear someone running up behind you. You whirl around in time to see a dirty man in rumpled clothes approaching you.

"Please!" he says, gasping for breath. "Please help me and my family. I need money badly!"

You look at your father, who shakes his head. When the homeless man finally leaves, your dad reminds you that a few dollars wouldn't really solve the man's problems and could be used to support a drinking or drug habit. *What can you do to help the homeless?*

Read 2 Corinthians 5:20. How are we Christ's ambassadors? What kind of "appeal" can He make through us, and how does He do it? Write out a list of the things you want your life to tell others about Christ.

Read Matthew 25:31-46. Think of several of the "least of these" in your own society, and create a modern-day parable or play based on these verses. Perform or read it at church or for your family.

Decide who "the least of these" is in your own school and do at least one thing this week to make that person's life more bearable.

We Are His Hands • Beyond the Edge

Specs: A hot and humid neighbor to Cambodia, Thailand is home to herds of western travelers, terraced rice paddies, modern cities and ancient ruins. Tigers, bears, waterfalls, bamboo forests, and wild orchids are some of the natural wonders of Thailand. Thai food is hot and sweet and full of spices. With more than 60 million people Thailand has a special need for missionaries, especially among the small mostly unreached people groups such as the Mien. Missionaries have a good amount of freedom despite a quota system that restricts the number of missionary visas in the country.

History: Since Europeans never colonized the area, Siam re-named itself Thailand meaning, "land of the free." Today millions of visitors travel to Thailand to visit its Buddhist monuments and lush jungles. Thailand has an agricultural and industrial base. Most of us probably remember noticing that something we own was "Made in Thailand."

People: The Thai people are generally very friendly and some-what modest. Thai is a tonal language like Chinese so it's a little hard to learn. There are several cultural groups spread throughout the country. One small group of people called the Mien, number around 16,000. They live, for the most part, in small enclaves sometimes no larger than a village.

A native girl in homemade clothes, carrying a homemade basket

DID YOU KNOW?

- You should never touch the head of anyone including children in Thailand. And never sit with your feet pointed at them, either.

- A Thai-Buddhist New Year's tradition calls for throwing water on anyone who passes by.

- There's an elephant roundup in the city of Surin every November!

- Have you ever seen "The king and I"? The Thai consider the movie an insult to their culture.

- Wat Trimitr is a monastery featuring a huge solid-gold Buddha.

- Royal barges are magnificent boats still used by the king for special occasions.

- To prove their water is boiled (drinkable), some restaurants add tea leaves that turn their water a very pale brown.

A village gamnon (chief) leads a celebration.

51

Brian and Duang Wilson, happy in Thailand

Hallelujah! By Brian Wilson

Brian closed the *Adventist Frontiers* magazine in frustration. "It hasn't moved!" he complained to Duang. "Our monthly pledge bar hasn't moved up at all."

Duang sighed. During the past months of their furlough she and Brian had been trying to raise enough financial support to return to Thailand. They had had very limited success, and now, in December, they still needed about $400 in commitments. (All AFM missionaries raise their own funds before they leave for their particular country. Usually, people commit to support a family on a monthly basis, thus becoming monthly "donors.")

"We should be leaving for Thailand soon," Brian told Marcy at the AFM office, "but we can't raise the money in such a short time. What should we do?"

Marcy listened quietly, then pulled out a sheet of paper covered with numbers.

"Brian," she began, "several of your largest donors have been forced to stop supporting you. And now that you and Duang are parents, your cost of living has risen even more. These numbers reflect the new amount you need to raise in monthly support." Marcy handed Brian the page, and his eyes quickly found the highlighted number at the bottom.

"One thousand dollars!" He nearly screeched the words. "That's impossible!" Months of built-up frustration threatened to explode in an angry speech. After a few quick words to Marcy, Brian left the office.

He rushed to their temporary apartment, but he couldn't stay inside for long. *Frustration is too small a word to describe my feelings right now!* Brian thought grimly as he yanked on his shoes. *How can AFM expect us to raise that much money? It's impossible. It's also impossible for us to continue working with AFM.*

Brian slammed the door and stepped outside. As he walked the gray tree-lined streets, Brian began a letter of resignation to AFM in his head. *I'll type it as soon as I go home,* he resolved. *It's time to get out of this ridiculous situation.*

But when Brian told Duang about his plans, she shook her head. "Why don't we try for one more month and see how God blesses?" she suggested. "If we still haven't raised the money at the end of the month, we can quit with confidence that the Lord is leading us in another direction."

Brian pondered this alternative. The resignation letter hovered temptingly in his mind. But he couldn't find any reasonable argument to counter Duang's proposal. "All right," he agreed reluctantly. "We'll try it for just one month."

Duang and Brian knelt in their tiny living room and committed themselves to trying their best to raise the necessary funds. "We leave the rest to You, God," Duang prayed with confidence. "We trust You for blessings and guidance."

The next several weeks were filled with phone calls, visits to strangers, and even trips to downtown business offices. Brian called friends, relatives, and people he hadn't seen in over 10 years. He walked door-to-door and asked for support. But although most people listened to his story, they seldom pledged more than $25 a month.

By the second week in January the situation had hardly improved. "You must go back to Thailand," Clyde Morgan, AFM's

Brian tells the story of Jonah to his young friends in Thailand.

director, told Brian. "You may have to leave Duang and baby Benya behind for now, but you must return to your people."

Reluctantly Brian made reservations to return to Thailand the following Tuesday. "We still have $600 left to raise in less than a week," he reminded Duang that evening. "Should I return to Thailand anyway?"

After more prayer and thought, Duang and Brian decided that if the Lord provided at least $400 of the $600 still needed by Monday afternoon, they would take it as a signal from Him that He wanted Brian to return to Thailand the next day. "If not, I'll stay here until we know what we should do," Brian promised. In his mind he added a private prayer. *Lord, if You really want us to go back to Thailand, please send a little more than $400 to confirm it. Thank You.*

Over the weekend Brian and Duang prayed constantly, ready to do whatever God suggested. Finally, on Monday afternoon they drove to the AFM office and asked how much money they had received.

To their surprise they had received not $400 (the amount they had asked for), not $600 (the amount they actually needed), but $800 in monthly pledges—all of which had come in over the weekend! Tears clouded their eyes as they thanked God for His blessings.

That night they celebrated as Brian packed for his return flight to Thailand. Although it would be a lonely few weeks until they were reunited overseas, both Brian and Duang felt at peace with their decision. God had shown them, beyond a shadow of a doubt, that He wanted them to stay in the mission field.

Why did I worry? Why did I doubt? Brian wondered as he packed. *I should have remembered that God always works things out according to His timing if we ask, trust, and put everything on the line for Him.*

Get Into the Action!

1. Why did Brian consider quitting AFM for good?
2. Read Romans 11:33-36. How could these verses have been a blessing to Brian and Duang as they tried to raise the funds to return to Thailand?
3. Why do you think God provided even more money than Brian and Duang prayed for?

Scenario

Your older brother, Sam, sets his guitar on its stand and begins picking up the songbooks. "I don't think I can do this," he confesses. "I can't keep leading the youth group when no one shows up for the meetings."

He gestures around the empty room. "I go to all the trouble of creating a program every week, and only two or three people show up to enjoy it. I promised God I'd try this out, but I think I've tried long enough. I'm going to quit to-morrow. It's just not worth the effort."

How can you help Sam in this situation?

Take Action!

Read and memorize Ezekiel 34:26. What hymn is based on this verse?

How has God showered you with blessings this past week?

How has He fulfilled His promises to you? Make a list of reasons to praise God, and use it when you pray tonight.

Read Psalm 23 as a prayer.

Hallelujah! • Beyond the Edge

52

David Dill

Beginnings By Jennifer G. Dill

David and Jennifer Dill agreed. It was time to begin a new teaching ministry in their village. Together they set the as the Chinese New Year target date for their new project. *It's here,* Jennifer thinks to herself as she begins decorating her house for the holiday. *This is the beginning of calling others to join us in following God.*

She steps back to look at the red paper she has hung on her front door. All the other Mien villagers decorate their doors with the same red paper and write Chinese characters on them, wishing visitors prosperity and health throughout the coming year. Jennifer smiles. Their red papers, however, call for all nations to come and worship the Lord. They call for God's praise to be sung by the whole world.

A tingle runs up Jennifer's spine. From this point on, everything will be different. She remembers the endless spirit ceremonies she and David have watched without comment. They can be silent no more. No longer will they quietly listen to their

Leader of Dills' Village

neighbors talk about throwing fire over their heads while in a deep trance, speaking as though their actions are the same as worshiping the true Creator God.

God is leading us to turn up the heat of evangelistic fire, Jennifer realizes again. *It's time for beginnings and change.* She wonders how soon the neighbors will notice their different attitude.

It doesn't take long to find out. Before long the Chinese daughter-in-law of a neighbor stops in for a visit.

"What is this?" she asks, squinting to make out the characters hung on the Dills' front door. Finally, something in her heart language! The woman steps still closer, excitement showing in the expression on her face and carefully reads the words about God. She walks inside without comment and immediately notices more banners hanging around a picture of Jesus, the Good Shepherd, in the living room. Later, the woman notices the Dills' Chinese Bible.

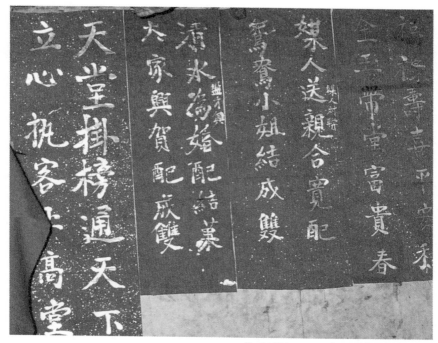

Taoist Chinese text for wedding ceremonies

"Can I take it home?" she asks eagerly. "I'd like to look at it more closely."

Jennifer's heart soars as she hands over the Bible. It is a beginning.

Not much later, another visitor stops by. Nai Wuon, the oldest woman in the village, makes her way up to the Dill's porch. Her stooped figure bends still lower to lay down her walking stick, then she sits on a short stool across from Jennifer. As their eyes meet, Jennifer realizes that Nai Wuon could die any day, and it would be without Jesus. Impressed, Jennifer goes to sit beside the old woman and talks with her about the things around them, which leads to Creation. Jennifer tells her briefly about the fall of man.

"Jesus came to throw away our sins and give us new life in Him," Jennifer explains carefully. To her surprise, Nai Wuon returns every few days to listen as she attempts to read aloud to her from the Mien Bible. It is a beginning.

San Yien and his wife come to visit later in the week. They are from another village and have come to see pictures that the Dills took of their recent wedding. During their conversation San asks a very important question.

"Do you have a Mien Bible in the English script?" he wonders out lout. "I am a Catholic and would like to read the Bible for myself."

Jennifer and David show him the Pentateuch that they have, and he works his way through a few words. His wife beams. He is far more able to read than others in the room. When the couple leaves, San takes the Pentatuch with him and agrees to visit again soon. It is a beginning.

Seven students from the Seventh-day Adventist academy in Chiang Mai return home for the holiday. "They look completely different than when they left!" Jennifer whispers to David as they troop toward the Dills' house. Increased health and intelligence is written upon their faces for all to see. Some show a deep interest in following God. They try to show up on Sabbath mornings to be taught more of the Bible. Although their parents still send them to the fields to work sometimes, it is still a beginning.

David and Jennifer give each student some Bible coloring books donated by students in Washington State. They use these books to tell parents and younger brothers and sisters the stories of the Bible. "Even my father will sit and listen for a long time!" one student reports excitedly. David and Jennifer smile. It is a beginning.

Later, when David and Jennifer walk up to the *Gamnon's* (chief's) house, he sits at the table, looking very tired and drained

"You go to town every day," Jennifer mentions. "You must be exhausted."

The gammon nods. "My life is hard. I lie down and can't sleep. I sit without comfort (or peace). I eat, and it doesn't taste good. My life has no peace." He turns to David and says, "You lie down and sleep long. You sit with comfort. You eat delicious food. Your life has peace." He goes on to say that his "god" doesn't give him peace.

Jennifer's heart races, and she sends up a quick prayer for

the gammon. He is starting to see something important. It is a beginning.

And the beginnings continue. David and Jennifer grow anxious to start small groups of people who read their Bibles each week and then meet to encourage each other. Since only one village member can read, they begin making tapes of someone reading the book of Genesis that they can use for these groups.

"Please, Lord," David and Jennifer pray each day. "Help this beginning to really take hold. Make many of our neighbors excited about the Bible story. This is an exciting place to be, but we know how much hard work lies ahead. Help us to be strong, and help others to pray for our work."

Cows are an important part of mountain village life.

1. Why do you think the gammon cannot find peace or satisfaction in his life?
2. David and Jennifer spent years before this time, simply getting to know the villagers and establishing their trust. Why do you think they waited so long to start this fresh beginning and tell people about Jesus?
3. How do you think the seven young students can be a real witness to their family members?

You have been friends with Carrie for several years now. You met at the pool one summer, and have enjoyed hanging out together ever since. Although you know Carrie is not a Christian, you have been reluctant to say anything about your faith. You didn't want to "scare her off." Now, however, she sits on your bed and stares at the Bible on your desk. "You're so much different than me," she says quietly. "Why do you study the Bible? Why do you go to church? What's it all about?" *How will you answer Carrie's questions?*

1. Students in Washington State sent Bible coloring books to Thailand. If something that small can be such a big witness, imagine what other things could help in the mission field! Make a list of things you have that might be useful overseas. Talk to you parents about sending a box to Thailand or some other country to help the missionaries there.
2. Think of a secular custom that is associated with each of these holidays: Christmas, Easter, and the New Year. Now, like David and Jennifer Dill, think of several ways you can change those customs to show that you are a Christian. Try them out when the holidays come around.
3. Read 2 Corinthians 5:20. How do you think God is making His "appeal" through you, one of His ambassadors? Pray every day for the next week that He will make you open to the things He wants you to do.